VERILOG BY EXAMPLE

A Concise Introduction for FPGA Design

VERILOG BY EXAMPLE

A Concise Introduction for FPGA Design

Blaine C. Readler

Full Arc
Press

VERILOG BY EXAMPLE
A Concise Introduction for FPGA Design

Published by Full Arc Press

Visit us at: http://www.readler.com

E-mail: blaine@readler.com

An acknowledgement and thanks to Lulu Enterprises, Inc. for making the publishing of this book possible.

http://www.lulu.com

ISBN: 978-0-9834973-0-1

Printed in the United States of America

First Edition: 2011

Dedicated to Chuck Rothrauff who first gave me a job designing with verilog
even though I knew nothing about verilog.

Contents

Introduction

This is the book I wish I'd had seventeen years ago when I tackled my first verilog design. The idea for this reference is to have you looking at workable examples by the shortest path possible. Like any descriptive language, whether verilog, VHDL, or C++, there are layers of features and capabilities that will ultimately be brought to bear if you use it long enough, but most of which can represent just a confusing distraction if introduced early on. This book initially strips away all but the very bare essentials to show you those fundamental aspects of the language that are universally required in almost any design. Later, it builds, feature-by-feature, more sophisticated capabilities.

The material is intended for students and engineers, both hardware and software, who already have a working knowledge of digital design and operation. It is not an instructional text on how to design logic. Additionally, it is intended to provide a very quick entry into verilog basics; it is not a comprehensive verilog reference. But I'm sure you didn't expect that for less than $20.

The contexts of the examples assume FPGAs (versus ASICs or, God forbid, discrete logic). This is by far the most ubiquitous use of HDL (Hardware Description Language) today. And in any case, if you're just learning HDL, it is highly unlikely that you've been hired to do ASIC development.

All examples used in this book are available as text files at:

http://www.readler.com

A note about punctuation: commas and periods are generally placed before closing parenthesis. For example, the following words might describe my approach to writing this book: "fastidious," "thorough," and "clarity." However, I have taken the liberty to break this rule throughout the following text in order to avoid confusion about the exact spelling of signal names. So, for example, in this context I might write that "in_1", "out_1", and "enable_b" comprise all the signals of block "mux_2".

The Tool Flow

This subject could be a whole book onto itself, but we will limit it here to just what's needed to see how verilog code is used. Verilog, like VHDL, is a hardware description language (HDL), and as such, completely describes how the logic design works. Along with a device-specific file defining implementation details such as device package type, I/O pin assignments, etc., the verilog code is all that's needed to create an operating FPGA. The "operating FPGA" is embodied in a binary object file that is loaded into the device after power-up. The tools described here are used to get from the verilog source code to this loadable binary object file.

Step 1: coding

This is simply the process of laying the ideas in your head down into verilog code, which is just a text file. If you've done software coding, you are completely familiar with this step. Any text editor will work, but professional text editors will help by color-coding syntax categories of verilog (assuming your version supports verilog);

Step 2: simulation

Although not strictly necessary to achieve a successfully compiled load file, simulation should be considered a practical requirement. Foregoing this step would be like spending months designing, building, and packing a parachute, and then jumping out of a plane without ever testing it. There is a finite possibility your design will work as intended—decreasing rapidly with complexity—but more than likely you will see the ground rushing up at you as you engage power and your FPGA does absolutely nothing.

Step 3: synthesis

The first two steps were your creative contribution. Step 3 begins the automated process of translating your text into operating logic. The synthesis step can be thought of as a bridge between your human text description and a gate-level representation. Gate-level here doesn't necessarily mean just AND and OR gates, but includes basic functional blocks as muxes and flip-flops. It is at this step that we find out if our code can be practically translated into logic that can be implemented in an FPGA. The output from the synthesis step looks very much like a netlist. Expensive stand-alone synthesis tools are often used for large or complex designs, but most FPGA vendor software includes synthesis that is quite adequate for many applications.

Step 4: compile

Whereas the synthesis of step 3 still comprises somewhat abstract logic constructs, the final compile step maps the synthesis netlist-like logic description into the specific logic and routing resources of the FPGA device. This step is always performed by the vendor software. We can define pins assignments, or let the tool automatically assign them (almost never done on all but the most difficult designs). It is in this compile step that we find out if the design that was synthesizable can actually be implemented into our chosen device. The output of the compile step is the binary load file that is used to configure the FPGA.

In and Out

First a word about coding style is necessary. What you find in this book are the author's methods developed over many years of practice. The goal should always be to produce readable code that is easy to understand. Different people have different preferences, though, and you will find as many individual styles as there are people coding. About the only absolutely wrong style is no style, i.e., where all the text is smashed to the left margin with no indenting or consistent parenthetical blocking. You should note that there are many shortcuts that could be taken with the code used throughout this book, but you'll never be wrong by including optional parenthesis or block flags, but you could very well cause your code to synthesize in an unintended manner if you make careless eliminations.

The synthesis tool expects certain standard file structures. We'll start with almost the simplest design possible in order to introduce the minimum requirements: two combinatorial operations on three inputs. Here's how it looks as logic block flow. Note that this box represents the entire FPGA.

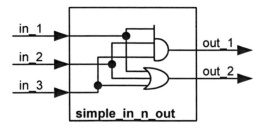

Simple In and Out

The verilog code can be seen on the next page. The text file implements one "module," which for this simple design is the entire design. The word "module" is a required keyword, and is followed by the name of the module. For our purposes, a module is always synonymous with a file, so the module name is the same as the file name. Note, though, that the module name has no file extension (which for verilog is always "v", e.g., "simple_in_n_out.v").

```
/////////////////////////////////////////////////
//
// Header information -- details about the context,
// constraints, etc..
//
/////////////////////////////////////////////////

module simple_in_n_out                    ← module / file name
        (
                 // Inputs
                 in_1,
                 in_2,
                 in_3,                              port list
                 // Outputs
                 out_1,
                 out_2
        ) ;

// Port definitions

input            in_1;
input            in_2;
input            in_3;                              I/O declarations

output           out_1;
output           out_2;

// ------------- Design implementation --------

assign out_1 = in_1 & in_2 & in_3;
assign out_2 = in_1 | in_2 | in_3;


endmodule
```

comment flags

Simple In and Out

A port list follows the name of the module, and defines all the signals in and out of the module, separated by commas. I/O declarations then follow, defining the direction of each signal listed in the port list (as we'll see later, new verilog versions allow the direction declarations to reside directly in the port list).

Following the declarations, the design proper begins. In this simplest case, the design consists of simple combinatorial assignments. Note that "assign" is a keyword, and indicates a combinatorial operation (also called a continuous assignment). An AND operation is indicated with "&," while "|" indicates an OR. The keyword "endmodule" marks the end of the verilog module (and also the text file here).

The synthesis software ignores everything after a comment flag—two forward slashes—to the end of the line.

The simple In and Out design just described defines outputs that are direct logical operations of inputs only. Virtually all practical designs, though, will have internal signals. We now introduce the simplest of these, the "wire," which is hardly nothing more than an intermediate stage of combinatorial processing. It is not misleading to think of it as an actual wire connecting internal gates. Note that a "wire" in verilog is technically a type of "net" entity, but in digital design it is common to refer to "wires," along with I/O and outputs of registers, collectively as simply all signals.

In the following example, note that the wire signal—here called "intermediate_sig"—must be declared as such before it is used. Although verilog allows signal declarations to be done anywhere in the design (before their use), it is standard practice to group them all at the beginning, usually just after the port I/O declarations.

Note that verilog is case sensitive. Some designers use this for effect, delineating similar signals by using the same name but different cases (e.g., the first letter, or the whole name). This is a very good technique if you want to confuse somebody trying to understand your code. If your goal is the opposite, I suggest avoiding this, and using a consistent case throughout.

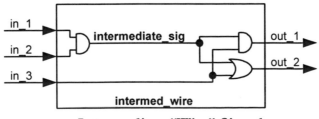

Intermediate "Wire" Signal

```
/////////////////////////////////////////////////
//
// Header information
// Intermediate Wire Signals
//
/////////////////////////////////////////////////

module intermed_wire
            (
                // Inputs
                in_1,
                in_2,
                in_3,
                // Outputs
                out_1,
                out_2
            );

    // Port definitions

    input           in_1;
    input           in_2;
    input           in_3;

    output          out_1;
    output          out_2;

    wire            intermediate_sig;

    // ------------- Design implementation --------

    assign intermediate_sig = in_1 & in_2;

    assign out_1 = intermediate_sig & in_3;
    assign out_2 = intermediate_sig | in_3;

endmodule
```

declarations

Intermediate "Wire" Signal

Verilog by Example

Logic designs often (usually) include multi-bit buses. These are represented in verilog as vector signals, and the width is defined in the declaration (single-bit signals are called scalars). The following example performs a combinatorial operation on two 4-bit input buses (AKA vectors) and a single-bit (AKA scalar) control signal.

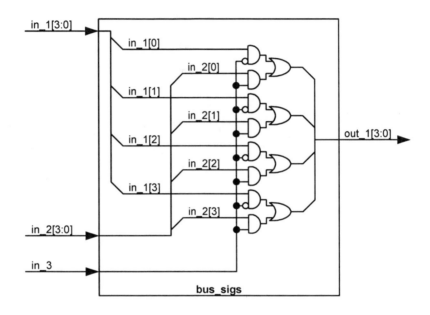

Bus Signals

Essentially, when "in_3" is low, then "in_1" is selected, and when "in_3" is high, "in_2" is selected. This is of course a two-input bus multiplexer.

Comparing the block flow diagram with the code on the following page, we can see that verilog vector representation of buses provides for compact representation (the logic for a whole bus is contained in one line). We also see, however, a mysterious intermediate "in_3_bus" signal. This is due to the manner of logical operation of the "&" and "|" operators (AND and OR). These perform bitwise operations, and expect the two values to be of equal bus size. Thus, the first assign statement extends the single-bit "in_3" to a 4-bit "in_3_bus", whereby all the bits of the new bus have the same value as the original "in_3". This is done using a replication operator, where the value of the signal inside the inner pair of braces is repeated the number of times as indicated by the number between the pairs of braces.

Note that "~" is a bitwise negation operator, i.e., it inverts each bit of the vector signal (bus "in_3_bus").

```
//////////////////////////////////////////////////
//
// Header information
// Bus Signals
//
//////////////////////////////////////////////////

module bus_sigs
            (
                // Inputs
                in_1,
                in_2,
                in_3,
                // Outputs
                out_1
            );

    // Port definitions

    input   [3:0]    in_1;
    input   [3:0]    in_2;
    input            in_3;
                                            This is replicated this many times.
    output  [3:0]    out_1;

    wire    [3:0]    in_3_bus;

    // ------------- Design implementation --------

    assign in_3_bus = {4{in_3}};
    assign out_1 = (~in_3_bus & in_1) | (in_3_bus & in_2);

endmodule
```

Bus Signals

11

Verilog by Example

The next block logic diagram shows the logic gates of the previous diagram collected together into a standard mux symbol. Note that we have not changed the function, just the representation.

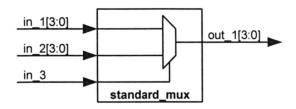

Standard Mux

The verilog code on the opposite page, although also functionally equivalent to the previous code, now reflects a different and more compact way of representing the multiplexer function. We here introduce verilog's combinatorial conditional construct, eliminating the "in_3_bus" intermediate signal of the previous example in the process. The assign statement reads as such: "when in_3_bus (the select control) is high, select in_2, else select in_1." This works very much like a limited version of the familiar IF/THEN statement of other languages.

Note that although a single instance of this conditional selection statement is used here, these can be concatenated. Here's an example:

```
assign  final_value =  select_1 ? input_1 :
                       select_2 ? input_2 :
                       select_3 ? input_3 :
                                  default_val;
```

Here, if "select_1" is high, "input_1" is selected, else if "select_2" is high, "input_2" is selected, else if "select_3" is high, "input_3" is selected, else "default_val" is selected. Note that a final default value must be included, otherwise the synthesis software will implement a (presumably unintended) latch.

```
//////////////////////////////////////////////
//
// Header information
// Standard Mux
//
//////////////////////////////////////////////
module standard_mux
          (
              // Inputs
              in_1,
              in_2,
              in_3,
              // Outputs
              out_1,
          );

    // Port definitions

    input   [3:0]   in_1;
    input   [3:0]   in_2;
    input           in_3;

    output  [3:0]   out_1;

    // ------------- Design implementation --------

    assign out_1 = in_3 ? in_2: in_1;

endmodule
```

Standard Mux

Finally, before we move beyond strictly combinatorial operation, we'll explore a few more details associated with buses. Where in the previous examples we selected entire buses for the output, here we break the buses out and then recombine them after some processing. Note that both input buses are four bits, but the output bus is six bits.

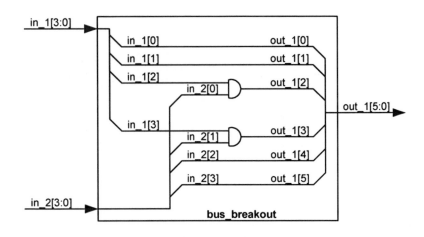

Bus Breakout

All of the combinatorial and bus reconstruction shown in the module above is implemented in one assignment in the code on the opposite page. Here we introduce bus concatenation, which is defined by a single set of braces. I have arranged the concatenation elements vertically on separate lines for clarity, but they could all be included on the same (albeit somewhat long) line, still separated by commas. Note that the MS element is always first (i.e., next to the left-most brace), while the LS element is always last (next to the right-most brace. Notice also that the first and last elements here comprise two bits, and that the two middle elements (each one bit) are the result of combinatorial operations.

```
//////////////////////////////////////////////
//
// Header information
// Bus Breakout
//
//////////////////////////////////////////////
module bus_breakout
            (
                // Inputs
                in_1,
                in_2,
                // Outputs
                out_1
            );

    // Port definitions
    input  [3:0]   in_1;
    input  [3:0]   in_2;
    output [5:0]   out_1;

    // ------------- Design implementation --------

    assign out_1 = { in_2[3:2],
                     (in_1[3] & in_2[1]),
                     (in_1[2] & in_2[0]),
                     in_1[1:0]
                   };

endmodule
```

                                              } concatenation

Bus Breakout

Verilog by Example

Clocks and Registers

In the introduction, I indicated that this book assumes that you have a working familiarity with digital design. The rubber is about to meet the road.

Clocked state logic comprises the vast majority of the workings of modern FPGAs, and it is here that the true complexity and sophistication of any hardware descriptive language unfolds. The fundamental principles of clocked operation in verilog, though, are straightforward, and easy to grasp if we take them a step at a time.

Until now, our code has consisted of continuous assignments, i.e., direct combinatorial logic. These "assign" statements are continuous in the sense that the output signal (the one being assigned) is continuously responsive to any and all inputs. Any input that changes (and is not gated off by the intervening logic) will immediately affect the output (ignoring physical delays). Contrary to this, registers hold or store information, and therefore require a different coding mechanism called a structured procedural statement. The most common structured procedural statement, and the one used almost exclusively for register implementations, is the "always block." There are a variety of flavors of this, but for implementation (i.e., synthesis) of clocked registers, we use exclusively the sequential, non-blocking version. That probably doesn't mean much to you, and that's okay for now. It is helpful to know that there are other forms in case you may happen across them, but for the time being, an always-block is synonymous with a register.

We'll begin by implementing the simplest form of a D-flop. Since this represents the basis for the various forms of registers we will continue to encounter, it is labeled as a "Reg." As shown in the timing diagram, output "out_1" follows "input in_1" at the clocked edges.

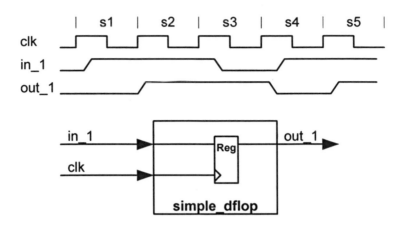

Simple D-flop

For the sake of brevity we've modified the file format a bit in the code on the opposite page (you'll get used to this as you look across different people's code).

We've added a new declaration for a "reg." This is necessary since we will be implementing output signal "out_1" as a register type. This is in contrast to the "wire" declaration. We have not previously needed to declare outputs explicitly as wires since in verilog outputs default to wire types (it wouldn't have been wrong to declare all the previous outputs as wires, just not necessary).

The section of code shown as the always-block implements the D-flop register. The information inside the parenthesis next to the "@" symbol is called the sensitivity list, and defines which signals can contribute to changes inside the block. Specifically, no activity inside the block can occur unless something in the sensitivity list changes. In the case of our simplest of D-flop registers, the sensitivity list contains just the clock signal. Further, "posedge" defines the flop as rising-edge triggered ("negedge" would be falling-edge triggered).

The operation is easy to see: at every rising clock edge (and only at a rising clock edge), the value of "in_1" is assigned to "out_1". You may wonder why we use the two-part "<=" symbol instead of a simple "=" for the assignment like we did with the combinatorial assignments, and the answer is that this defines it as a non-blocking assignment. This allows individual elements of more complex always-block structures to operate independently, but the important point is that all synthesized registers use this non-blocking assignment, so get used to it.

The "begin" and "end" lines define the body of the always-block. In this case where there is only one assignment line, the begin/end pair is actually optional, but I recommend always using them for consistency.

```
/////////////////////////////////////////////////
// Simple D-flop
/////////////////////////////////////////////////

module simple_dflop  (  clk,
                        in_1,
                        out_1
                     );

    input           clk;
    input           in_1;
    output          out_1;

    reg             out_1;

    // ------------ Design implementation --------

    always @ ( posedge clk )
      begin
        out_1 <= in_1;
      end

endmodule
```

                                                  } always block

Simple D-flop

Next we add an asynchronous reset to our simple D-flop. The timing diagram shows the operation where "reset" forces "out_1" low immediately during state s3, and "out_1" then remains low until clocked again back high at state s5.

Our convention will be that asynchronous controls (resets and presets) will enter the register box at the top or bottom, while all synchronous controls will connect to the front.

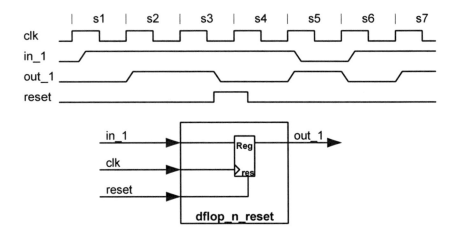

D-flop with reset

In the code on the opposite page you can see that the always-block has now grown to accommodate the reset. Since the reset is asynchronous and results in activity immediately, it must be included in the sensitivity list. Tagging it as "posedge" means that it will be high-active—the flop resets as soon as the reset goes high, but after the reset is lifted, the flop doesn't change until the next clock edge, thus only the rising edge of the reset requires immediate attention.

The body of the always-block has now become more complicated as we introduce if/else conditional statements to accommodate the reset. Any time "reset" his high, "out_1" is forced to zero. Since this happens as soon as reset goes active (reset is part of the sensitivity list), and at every rising clock edge, you can see that this effects an asynchronous clear. When reset is not high, then the "else" original in-to-out register assignment is selected (occurring only at rising clock edges).

Note that the reset zero assignment is made with " 1'b0 ". Verilog uses a specific format for static values. The first field defines the number of bits (i.e., the width of the vector), the next field, separated by the apostrophe, defines the radix, and the last field defines the actual value. Since in this case we have a simple one-bit zero, the first field is "1", and we let the value be defined as binary.

```
/////////////////////////////////////////////
// D-flop with reset
/////////////////////////////////////////////

module dflop_n_reset   (   clk,
                           reset,
                           in_1,
                           out_1
                       ) ;

    input         clk;
    input         reset;
    input         in_1;
    output        out_1;

    reg           out_1;

    // -------- Design implementation --------

    always @ ( posedge clk or posedge reset )
      begin
        if ( reset )
          out_1 <= 1'b0;
        else
          out_1 <= in_1;
      end

endmodule
```

D-flop with reset

Pressing on, we now add more functionality to our nascent register. Here we introduce two synchronous controls: an enable, and a low-active synchronous clear. We forgo a timing diagram since the operation is self-evident.

Note that the asynchronous reset remains. Besides benefiting from simple consistency, this demonstrates an important point about FPGA design in general: we invariably choose one reset method (synchronous or asynchronous), which is then used globally on all the registers. At a minimum, global resets are necessary for simulation, but additionally may be a practical necessity for proper testing in-circuit. In our case, we will always be using a global asynchronous reset. We should also note that on very large and/or fast designs, the global reset may be segmented into functional domains, but the premise that every flop shares a (semi)common reset remains.

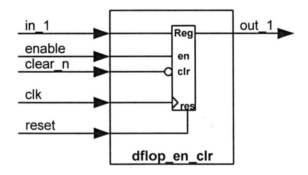

D-flop with enable and clear

The always-block in the code on the opposite page expands with the additional synchronous control functions. The asynchronous reset still takes priority (it comes first), but now a low "clear" signal will also force the output to zero as well. However, since this clear signal is not included in the sensitivity list, the change occurs at the next rising clock edge (thus, rendering it synchronous).

Notice that the "else if" conditional expression uses a logical equality test, whereas the "if" reset line did not. This is because the conditional expression is evaluated as either Boolean true or false. When "reset" is a one, its Boolean equivalent is by definition true.

The conditional expression can be as complicated as you like, spanning many lines of code, as long as the synthesis tool is able to determine a final Boolean result.

The final conditional statement implements the clock enable, and here again, since "enable" is high-active, no logic equality test is necessary. Notice that there is no final "else" statement. If there were, the latching operation of the clock enable would be defeated.

As with most other languages, the order of the conditional statements determines the priority.

```
////////////////////////////////////////////////
// D-flop with enable and clear

module dflop_en_clr  (   clk,
                         reset,
                         in_1,
                         enable,
                         clear,
                         out_1
                     );

    input           clk;
    input           reset;
    input           in_1;
    input           enable;
    input           clear;
    output          out_1;

    reg             out_1;

    // ----- Design implementation -------

    always @ ( posedge clk or posedge reset )
      begin
        if ( reset )
          out_1 <= 1'b0;
        else if ( clear == 1'b0 )
          out_1 <= 1'b0;
        else if ( enable )
          out_1 <= in_1;
      end

endmodule
```

D-flop with enable and clear

Verilog by Example

We now introduce a few common state-type operations to show how increasingly sophisticated register-based functions are implemented in always-blocks. A four-bit counter is enabled by a "start" event, and stopped by a "stop" event. The SR flop allows the start and stop events to be short, e.g. one-clock pulses, rather than a continuously enabling flag. Additionally, for further illustration, we delay the start signal two clocks and send it out.

You'll notice that we have not shown the asynchronous reset. This is done for clarity; from this point forward it is assumed. It is implemented in the code, and always will be (in this book).

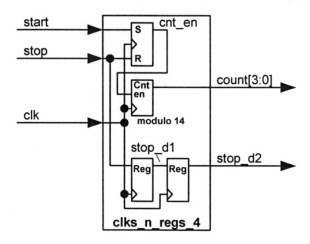

SR flop and counter

The code includes two register declarations for internal signals (cnt_en and stop_d1), and two register declarations for the two external signals (count[3:0] and stop_d2). We now have multiple always-blocks. Note that always-blocks operate concurrently, meaning they run simultaneously, independent of each other, just like two registers in a design.

Each always-block is associated with a coherent register function: one for the SR flop, one for the counter, and one for the two delays. The SR flop always-block needs no explanation beyond noting that there is no "else" statement, resulting in a latch function (which is indeed what we desire). The counter always-block also has no "else" statement, but since it is an enabled counter, it is also in a sense a latch. Notice that since the counter is modulo 14, the first "else if" statement clears it when the count is 13. A couple of things to note here: " 4'd13 " indicates a decimal thirteen, and we're now using a double "&&" in the conditional expression. This is because "&&" is a Boolean AND (versus the bitwise "&"), which is required for the conditional decision. In the same sense, "||" is a Boolean OR (versus the bitwise "|"). Note that we use " 4'h0 " for clearing the counter. This indicates a hex zero. It could just as well have been 4'b0000, or 4'd0. Similarly, the 4'd13 modulo rollover could have been the slightly less readable 4'hD, or even 4'b1101.

```
/////////////////////////////////////////
// SR flop and counter
/////////////////////////////////////////
module srflop_n_cntr (   clk,
                         reset,
                         start,
                         stop,
                         count
                     );

    input           clk;
    input           reset;
    input           start;
    input           stop;
    output [3:0]    count;

    reg             cnt_en;
    reg [3:0]       count;
    reg             stop_d1;
    reg             stop_d2;

    // ------ Design implementation -----

    // SR flop
    always @( posedge clk or posedge reset )
      begin
        if ( reset )
          cnt_en <= 1'b0;
        else if ( start )
          cnt_en <= 1'b1;
        else if ( stop )
          cnt_en <= 1'b0;
      end
```

```
// Counter
always @( posedge clk or posedge reset )
  begin
    if ( reset )
      count <= 4'h0;
    else if (    cnt_en
             && count == 4'd13
            )
      count <= 4'h0;
    else if ( cnt_en )
      count <= count + 1;
  end

// delay
always @( posedge clk or posedge reset )
  begin
    if ( reset )
      begin
        stop_d1 <= 1'b0;
        stop_d2 <= 1'b0;
      end
    else
      begin
        stop_d1 <= stop;
        stop_d2 <= stop_d1;
      end
  end
endmodule
```

SR flop and counter

The last always-block implements the two sequential delays. The points to note here are that multiple register signals can be grouped into the same always-block (when it makes sense), and that additional begin/end block boundaries are needed around each pair of signal assignments. Without these, the synthesis software might interpret, for example, that "stop_d2 <= stop_1" is not associated with the "else," but stands alone.

Finally, we should note that the three always-blocks could be collected together into one. This is shown on the next page.

```
always @ ( posedge clk or posedge reset )
  begin
    if ( reset )
      begin
        cnt_en  <= 1'b0;
        count   <= 4'h0;
        stop_d1 <= 1'b0;
        stop_d2 <= 1'b0;
      end
    else
      begin
        if ( start )
          cnt_en <= 1'b1;
        else if ( stop )
          cnt_en <= 1'b0;

        if (    cnt_en
             && count == 4'd13
           )
          count <= 4'h0;
        else if ( cnt_en )
          count <= count + 1;

        stop_d1 <= stop;
        stop_d2 <= stop_d1;
      end
  end
```

SR flop and counter, one always-block

This of course results in more compact code, but the benefit comes with a danger. Extreme care must be taken to make sure there is no ambiguity about what goes with what. If there's any doubt, begin/end block groupings are always available for clarifications.

Verilog by Example

State Machines

Everybody loves state machines, particularly people trying to understand your design. But the clarity is only as effective as how well the coding language communicates the state machine's structure. As we'll see, if coded with proper care to outline the operation, verilog provides a very good vehicle.

We'll use a fairly simple machine to demonstrate how they can be coded in verilog. After receiving a "go" event, the state machine transitions from the "idle" state to "active," where it waits while an auxiliary counter steps through a hundred clocks. Once this defined active duration is complete, the state machine returns to "idle," but passes through one last "finish" state on the way. This "finish" state produces a one-clock pulse on the "done" output signal. An external "kill" signal can terminate the wait active duration, forcing the state machine back to idle. For the sake of stability, though, the state machine waits in an "abort" state until the kill signal goes back inactive.

Note that this design assumes that the inputs are synchronized to the clock that drives the FPGA. Otherwise, the inputs would need to be clocked through an input register (i.e., synchronized) before presentation to the state machine to prevent spurious operation. In fact, if the extra state latency is not an issue, inputs are often re-clocked as standard procedure.

The "done" register is included to avoid combinatorial decode glitches. Gray or one-hot state coding could be used instead, but including an output register provides a more universal application.

You may recognize that the entire operation of this sample design could be implemented with just the counter alone (enabling and clearing it directly with the external signals), but the state machine presents a clear communication of the intent of the circuit, and also provides an easy avenue for later changes or expansion.

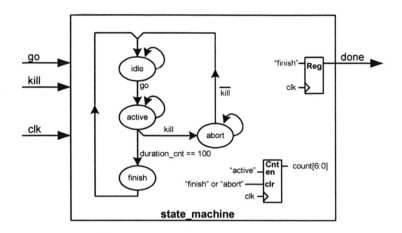

State Machine

```
//////////////////////////////////////
// State Machine

module state_machine_1 ( clk,
                         reset,
                         go,
                         kill,
                         done
                       );

    input           clk;
    input           reset;
    input           go;
    input           kill;
    output          done;

    reg [6:0]       count;
    reg             done;
    reg [1:0]       state_reg;

    // state machine parameters
    parameter    idle    = 2'b00;
    parameter    active  = 2'b01;
    parameter    finish  = 2'b10;
    parameter    abort   = 2'b11;
```

```verilog
    // ------ Design implementation -----

    // State Machine
    always @( posedge clk or posedge reset )
      begin
        if ( reset )
          state_reg <= idle;
        else
          case ( state_reg )
            idle :
              if ( go )               state_reg <= active;

            active :
              if ( kill )             state_reg <= abort;
              else if
                 (count == 7'd100) state_reg <= finish;

            finish :                  state_reg <= idle;

            abort :
              if ( !kill )            state_reg <= idle;

            default :                 state_reg <= idle;
          endcase
      end

    // Counter
    always @( posedge clk or posedge reset )
      begin
        if ( reset )
          count <= 7'h00;
        else if (    state_reg == finish
                  || state_reg == abort
                  )
          count <= 7'h00;
        else if ( state_reg == active )
          count <= count + 1;
      end

    // done register
    always @( posedge clk or posedge reset )
      begin
        if ( reset )
          done <= 1'b0;
        else if ( state_reg == finish )
          done <= 1'b1;
        else
          done <= 1'b0;
      end
endmodule
```

State Machine

31

Verilog by Example

State machines have limited effectiveness if we are not able to use human-friendly labels, and verilog provides two mechanisms for this. We will be using parameters to bridge alphanumeric state labels with numeric-coded states. As we'll see later, parameters are also often used in verilog designs to carry configuration information down into hierarchical sub-modules, but the advantage they offer for state machine labeling is the fact that they operate locally, i.e., unless specifically communicated into the module, the parameter's value is not affected by other parameter assignments in other modules. So, in general, the same parameter name can be used in different modules, and they will operate independently of each other.

This is not the case for the other possible mechanism for state machine labels: define statements. Unlike parameters, defines are global, meaning that a define assignment in another module could override one in yours. This, of course, could be disastrous if the override is done unintentionally just because the same name happened to be chosen for two unrelated defines.

In the code above, you can see that using parameter assignments we've associated the four states of our design with four distinct numerical (binary) values. We use two bits because that is all we need to define our four states. It would not be wrong to choose a wider bit field, and would provide the modest advantage that the machine would be easier to expand later. An important point is that the parameter assignments are for convenience of labeling only; the actual machine is implemented using a register vector—the two-bit "state_reg" in our case.

The first always-block implements the state machine using a case statement. Case statements are familiar if you have experience with almost any type of programming, but in a nutshell, the case statement selects and executes the statement group (identified with a following colon) that matches the value inside the parenthesis ("state_reg" in this example). Since the case statement is contained inside a clocked always-block, an assessment and one selected group is executed each clock.

We'll follow through some of the operation for demonstration. We start with the state machine in the idle state, where "state_reg" contains "idle" (2'b00). Each clock, the case selection executes the idle group, where if "go" is not high (not active) then nothing is done, so that for the next clock "state_reg" still contains "idle." Eventually "go" transitions high, and "state_reg" is assigned "active". This corresponds to the first transition of the state machine. For the next clock, the case statement selects for execution the "active" group, where "state_reg" remains unchanged until either "kill" goes high, or the counter reaches its terminal value (decimal 100), when the state machine then transitions to "abort" or "finish" respectively.

We'll not detail the entire machine operation, as you've surely gotten the gist by now. Note, however, that "!" is used to indicate "not kill." This is the same as " kill == 1'b0 ". Like the double "&&" and "||", "!" is a logical operator, and is normally used in conditional expressions. The "~" symbol (a bitwise negation) is usually used in combinatorial assignments. Since the results are often the same, designers sometimes use them indiscriminately.

We'll now review the coding structure. Normally the assignment statement (e.g. "state_reg <= active") follows the conditional statement on the next line. Here, though, we have it following on the same line. Verilog doesn't care, and this allows for a visually coherent form—the state machine operation is easily understood based on the transition decisions. We note that this is only possible because this always-block contains nothing but the state machine. If it didn't (as we'll soon see), then we would have to block multiple assignments with begin/end borders, ruining the regular matrix structure.

Finally, be aware that many synthesis programs require the default statement, even if the case statement already includes all possible selection branch combinations (considered "full"). The label "default" is a keyword (it was not defined as a parameter).

The counter and output register of this module are similar to those we've already looked at. Note that we decode state machine states directly in these blocks using the "state_reg" register signal and the state parameters. Also note that the "done" output is set to one based on a conditional "else if" test of the state machine. Most newer synthesis tools allow a more direct form:

```
always @( posedge clk or posedge reset )
  begin
    if ( reset )
      done <= 1'b0;
    else
      done <= ( state_reg == finish );
  end
```

Here the Boolean result of the state register comparison is translated to a binary bit for assignment to "done."

As we've noted, verilog code can be structured in a variety of ways. Some designers might prefer the auxiliary counter and output register to be collected into one always block along with the state machine. This is how it might look:

```
/////////////////////////////////////////
// State Machine

module state_machine_2 ( clk,
                         reset,
                         go,
                         kill,
                         done
                       );

    input       clk;
    input       reset;
    input       go;
    input       kill;
    output      done;

    reg [6:0]   count;
    reg         done;
    reg [1:0]   state_reg;

    // state machine parameters
    parameter   idle    = 2'b00;
    parameter   active  = 2'b01;
    parameter   finish  = 2'b10;
    parameter   abort   = 2'b11;

    // ------ Design implementation -----

    // State Machine
    always @( posedge clk or posedge reset )
      begin
        if ( reset )
          begin
            state_reg <=  idle;
```

```
            count      <= 7'h00;
            done       <=  1'b0;
          end
        else
          case ( state_reg )

            idle :
              begin
                count <= 7'h00;
                done  <= 1'b0;
                if ( go )
                   state_reg <= active;
              end

            active :
              begin
                count <= count + 1;
                done  <= 1'b0;
                if ( kill )
                   state_reg <= abort;
                else if ( count == 7'd100 )
                   state_reg <= finish;
              end

            finish :
              begin
                count      <= 7'h00;
                done       <= 1'b1;
                state_reg <= idle;
              end

            abort :
              begin
                count <= 7'h00;
                done  <= 1'b0;
                if ( !kill )
                   state_reg <= idle;
              end

            default :
              begin
                count      <= 7'h00;
                done       <= 1'b0;
                state_reg <= idle;
              end
          endcase
      end
endmodule
```

State Machine, one always-block

Besides losing the visual advantage of correlating the state machine decisions with corresponding actions, this type of code structure is susceptible to mis-operation if care isn't taken to account for every register state in every case selection. Although often resulting in code that is not as tight, when each function is implemented with its own always-block, each operation is clear and concise.

Modular Design

The design examples we've used so far have been very small for obvious reasons. Designs of increasing complexity reach a point where containing them in a single file becomes cumbersome. At some point sheer size compels us to break up the design into component parts, possibly multiple layers of hierarchy.

There are other good reasons besides just size, though, to use a modular approach:

o reuse (components of a design can be used in multiple places without repeating all the code details);

o pre-existing designs (code developed elsewhere can be incorporated as a "black box" without caring about constituent details);

o clarity (the code can be segmented into functional pieces that correspond to blocks described in high level descriptions);

o simulation (individual pieces of the design can be often times be simulated more rigorously and completely than when embedded in the larger operation);

o changes (by compartmentalizing the functioning, the consequences of changes can be studied and simulated in isolation).

Now having effused about the benefits of modular design, we immediately offer caution against overuse. Keep in mind that anyone examining your code will need to navigate through as many files as there are modules. No one will love you if you break out every register, mux, and counter as its own instantiated module, when the associated always-block would have taken no more room than the instantiated module that's replacing it.

With that admonishment out of the way, we can proceed to look at how modules are instantiated within other modules.

For the first example, we will use the module design from the previous section (State Machines) for our internal instantiated module. Note that there were two coded versions of that, but since they operate exactly the same, and have the same input/outputs, we could use either one.

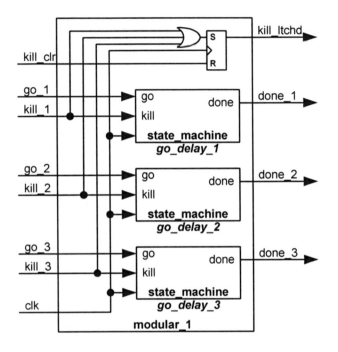

First Modular Example

Here, we've instantiated three copies of the state_machine module in a new higher-level module (sometimes called a "wrapper" when most of the code consists of instantiated sub-modules) called "modular_1". We've labeled the first instantiated copy as "go_delay_1", the second as "go_delay_2", and the third as "go_delay_3". Additionally, we've also added an SR latch to detect if any of the modules' internal counts were "killed," and have provided a signal (kill_clr) to clear the latch.

On the next page is the code file for "modular_1".

```
/////////////////////////////////////
// Modular Design #1

module modular_1 (   clk,
                     reset,
                     go_1,
                     kill_1,
                     go_2,
                     kill_2,
                     go_3,
                     kill_3,
                     kill_clr,
                     done_1,
                     done_2,
                     done_3,
                     kill_ltchd
              );

     input          clk;
     input          reset;
     input          go_1;
     input          kill_1;
     input          go_2;
     input          kill_2;
     input          go_3;
     input          kill_3;
     input          kill_clr;

     output         done_1;
     output         done_2;
     output         done_3;
     output         kill_ltchd;

     reg            kill_ltchd;

     // ------ Design implementation -----

     // first module instantiation
     state_machine_1 go_delay_1
            (
               .reset   ( reset  ),
               .clk     ( clk    ),
               .go      ( go_1   ),
               .kill    ( kill_1 ),
               .done    ( done_1 )
            );

     // second module instantiation
     state_machine_1 go_delay_2
            (
               .reset   ( reset  ),
```

```
                    .clk       ( clk    ),
                    .go        ( go_2   ),
                    .kill      ( kill_2 ),
                    .done      ( done_2 )
                );

        // third module instantiation
        state_machine_1 go_delay_3
            (
                    .reset     ( reset  ),
                    .clk       ( clk    ),
                    .go        ( go_3   ),
                    .kill      ( kill_3 ),
                    .done      ( done_3 )
                );


        // Kill Latch
        always @( posedge clk or posedge reset )
          begin
            if ( reset )
              kill_ltchd <= 1'b0;
            else if (    kill_1
                      || kill_2
                      || kill_3
                    )
              kill_ltchd <= 1'b1;
            else if ( kill_clr )
              kill_ltchd <= 1'b0;
          end

    endmodule
```

First Modular Example

The entire module design consists of three lower-level module instantiations, followed by one always-block for the SR latch. Each module instantiation includes:

o the name of the instantiated module (state_machine_1);

o followed by a label (e.g., "go_delay_1" or "go_delay_2");

o and a port connection list, where the connections are made between the instantiat-ing module and the instantiat-ed module.

A period precedes each port signal of the instantiat-ed module, while the connecting signal of the instantiat-ing module follows inside parenthesis. Note that each connection signal pair is separated by a comma.

Keep in mind that the instantiat-<u>ing</u> name of the instantiat-<u>ed</u> module (state_machine_1) must match exactly that of the instantiat-<u>ed</u> module (and therefore the actual file name, minus the ".v" extension). It often happens that multiple versions of a file may have the same name, located in different folders. You will explicitly tell the synthesis software where the one you want to use resides.

Next, we make a minor change to our example modular design. Each module stage now ORs its "go" input with the previous stage's "done" output.

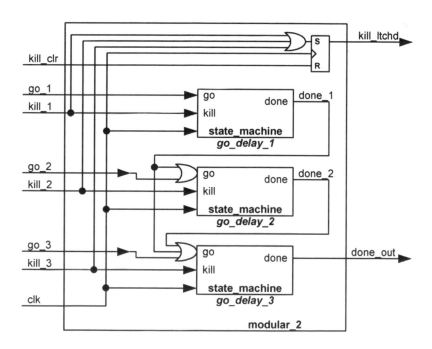

Second Modular Example

```
/////////////////////////////////////////
// Modular Design #2

module modular_2 (  clk,
                    reset,
                    go_1,
                    kill_1,
                    go_2,
                    kill_2,
                    go_3,
                    kill_3,
                    kill_clr,
                    done_out,
                    kill_ltchd
                 );

    input       clk;
    input       reset;
    input       go_1;
    input       kill_1;
    input       go_2;
    input       kill_2;
    input       go_3;
    input       kill_3;
    input       kill_clr;

    output      done_out;
    output      kill_ltchd;

    reg         kill_ltchd;
    wire        done_1;
    wire        done_2;

    // ------ Design implementation -----

    // first module instantiation
    state_machine_1 go_delay_1
            (
               .reset   ( reset  ),
               .clk     ( clk    ),
               .go      ( go_1   ),
               .kill    ( kill_1 ),
               .done    ( done_1 )
            );

    // second module instantiation
    state_machine_1 go_delay_2
            (
               .reset   ( reset  ),
               .clk     ( clk    ),
               .go      ( done_1 | go_2 ),
```

```
              .kill    ( kill_2 ),
              .done    ( done_2 )
          );

      // third module instantiation
      state_machine_1 go_delay_3
          (
              .reset   ( reset    ),
              .clk     ( clk      ),
              .go      (    done_1
                        | done_2
                        | go_3
                       ),
              .kill    ( kill_3   ),
              .done    ( done_out )
          );


      // Kill Latch
      always @( posedge clk or posedge reset )
        begin
          if ( reset )
            kill_ltchd <= 1'b0;
          else if (    kill_1
                    || kill_2
                    || kill_3
                   )
            kill_ltchd <= 1'b1;
          else if ( kill_clr )
            kill_ltchd <= 1'b0;
        end

  endmodule
```

Second Modular Example

Notice that the "done_1" and "done_2" outputs of the first example design now become wires. This is necessary since every signal (i.e., net) must be declared. As we learned earlier, the original "done_1" and "done_2" outputs were also wires by default. Once we remove the output declarations, though, we must now explicitly declare them as wires.

The second point to notice is that we've performed the inter-stage ORing right inside the port connection list. Isn't verilog cool?

(As a minor point, you might look at how we've structured the ORing differently for the second and third stages).

Verilog by Example

Instantiated modules are not limited to your own verilog code, or even to code that was written by another designer of your acquaintance. Instantiating sub-modules is the method we use to incorporate a variety of functionality delivered as tested and documented components. These include "IP cores"—code, sometimes quite substantial and complex, provided (often sold) by third-parties that implement a well-defined set of functions. Common examples of cores are complete micro-processors. You could, if you wanted, include a PowerPC™ in your design. Other examples of off-the-shelf cores are PCI interfaces, video encoder/decoders, encryption blocks for data security (e.g., DES and AES), and error detection/correction (e.g., Viterbi and Reed-Solomon). There are probably as many IP cores as there are useful segmentable functions. Many are available from the FPGA vendor directly. Some are fixed, straight-forward functional blocks, such as 8b/10b encoder/decoders. Others are synthesized based on designer-provided parameters during the design process by vendor-specific software that comes integrated as part of the FPGA vendor's tool suite, or purchased separately. Examples of these sorts of cores are FFT and FIR filter DSP blocks, Gigabit Ethernet interfaces, and FIFOs.

Another important class of vendor-provided modules is primitive cores. These are functionally simpler blocks that are either built directly into the FPGA device fabric, or are synthesized in a way that utilizes fabric specifics that would not otherwise be visible to general third-party synthesis tools (thus the label primitive). The key difference between primitive cores and the afore-described off-the-shelf IP cores is that, whereas the latter generally consist of verilog code that becomes a part of the overall synthesized design, primitive cores are just place-markers in the code that the vendor compiler (versus the synthesis stage) recognizes and inserts the proper functionality at the device-specific stage of the path towards a final binary build file. These place-markers are called "black boxes," and have the appearance in the code of a normal instantiated module. However, no associated verilog file exists to go along with them. In fact, most synthesis software upon encountering an instantiated module for which it cannot find an associated verilog file will automatically declare it as a black box entity. Designers, as a result, must routinely scan synthesis results looking for instances of black box declarations in case they are simply the result of lost or misplaced verilog files.

Primitive cores will be addressed again in the next section on memories.

A final word about module instantiations, and we tread here with trepidation. We have shown you how to make inter-module port connections using a connection list, where each instantiat-ed module's I/O port is paired with an instantiat-ing module's signal. There is no ambiguity in this: each port is specifically identified with its associated signal. However . . . verilog does allow another short-cut method, called an "ordered list." Here, only the instantiat-ing module's signals are listed, and the instantiat-ed module's I/O ports are inferred based on their position. An ordered list module instantiation from the previous code might look like this:

```
// first module instantiation, using an ordered list
go_delay_1 state_machine_1
        ( reset, clk, go_1, kill_1 , done_1 );
```

Now that we've revealed this, it's like cracking the top of Pandora's Box. You can see the attraction—simple and short; but also prone to mistakes. In fact, I go so far as to consider this method a trap waiting to be sprung. The reason is that port misconnections are not obvious, and if the mismatched port types are the same, then the synthesis tool will not flag a problem. Mismatches can happen if, for example, modifications are made to the instantiat-ed module that cause the ordering of the port list to change (remember that often the instantiat-ed module is not under your control). Worse still, verilog allows you to leave unconnected output ports of instantiat-ed modules out of the port list. This means that if, for example, a new output signal is added to your instantiat-ed module (this happens quite often), shifting down all the original signals, and if the last signal is an output, it is now unconnected (and signals above are misconnected), but no error flag is raised by the tools.

I urge you to resist.

Verilog by Example

Memories

Memories are an important component in many fields of digital design, and they come in a variety of forms: DRAM, SDRAM, DDR, QDR, SRAM, FIFO, LIFO, DP, etc.. Of these, the first four are of course not (yet) available for FPGA implementation, but almost any other form imaginable has probably been implemented. Memory design in FPGAs is another topic that could be a whole book unto itself, and here we will simply review the fundamentals of designing memories using verilog.

Memories implemented in FPGAs (versus memory controllers, which would also include the DRAMs, etc.) can be defined in three general ways:

1) infer the memory directly via the verilog code;

2) build the memory using the vendor's primitive RAM structures;

3) design the memory using the FPGA vendor's specialized tools.

We'll discuss the last two first. The second option (primitive RAM structures) uses RAM resources that are built into the FPGA device fabric, and thus are the most efficient means of building memory functions (and if you don't use them, then they represent valuable substrate that goes unused). Each RAM block occupies a fixed amount of FPGA die, and they usually have a limited degree of flexibility as to their depth versus width (aspect ratio). These RAM blocks are an example of primitive cores discussed in the previous section, and as explained there, when using these in a verilog design, they are instantiated as black box modules. In this mode, it's up to you the designer to build up in verilog any associated control logic, such as circular addressing for FIFOs, logic for the FIFO depth flags, etc.. Most built-in FPGA RAM blocks can be configured to operate as dual-port memories, vastly simplifying many designs.

Verilog by Example

The third option (vendor's specialized tools) is by far the easiest approach, particularly with application-specific FIFOs. This method was also discussed in the previous section, and functional blocks built around memories (FIFOs, ROMs, CAMs, etc.) are just an example of the IP cores built using vendor-specific software. The designer, via the GUIs of the vendor software, establishes the parameters of the memory functional block. Parameters for FIFOs, for example, might include depth, input width, output width, various flag locations, etc..

The main downside to using vendor-supplied IP core generators is that they depend on vendor-supplied software. This limits the design's portability, meaning that, should the design be moved to another vendor's device (e.g., migrate to an ASIC), all those IP cores will need to be re-designed, either using the new vendor's IP generation tool, or built up anew in verilog. Either way, this often translates to a major design and test effort. If, on the other hand, you are confident you will never change FPGA vendors, then this is not an issue.

However, even if you never change FPGA vendors, there still may be issues related to the vendor's IP generation tool evolution. If you knew that you were going to create the design just once and never revisit it again, there would be no problem. But in practice, this almost never happens. Whether from requirement changes introduced later, or subtle problems found down the road that require modifications, inevitably the design sees changes. If the changes manifest in one of the vendor-generated cores, then the IP module will need to be re-generated, and this in turn may require you to use a newer version of the vendor core generation tool. Although rare, there sometimes are differences in how the new tool creates the functions, particularly when the vendor replaces a whole category subset of the tool with a completely "new and improved" version. Also, again though rare, a vendor may completely eliminate support for an esoteric, infrequently used type of core.

Lastly, we go back to the first method of defining memories: inferring the memory directly via the verilog code. This is the method used when the design is expected, or even suspected, to migrate later to an ASIC, where RAM blocks and convenient GUI-based vendor IP generators are but a rumor. Also, inferred memories are often used for very small memories—specifically, memories significantly smaller than the smallest primitive RAM block (we may be saving those for places where they are really needed).

First, we should explain why we say that the memory is "inferred," and not just implemented in the code like a register or mux. Synthesis tools—whether FPGA or ASIC—include specialized capabilities to recognize when a memory is being implied (AKA inferred). The reason is that the tool can then take advantage of those memory resources at its disposal (specific to the chosen device). In the case of FPGAs, this may ensure that the synthesis tool uses RAM blocks if appropriate (and allowed by the user). Even if primitive IP blocks are not used, the synthesis tool may take special precautions (e.g., coordinated timing) when constructing a memory from verilog code, but only if it recognizes it as such.

Each synthesis tool may have its own particular requirements associated with inferred memories, but one aspect that virtually all have in common is that they expect the memory to be implemented as an array of registers. Verilog has a specific declaration and syntax usage for register arrays. Here's an example of a register array declaration:

```
reg [7:0]   mem_buf[0:127];
```

This declaration defines an array of 128 8-bit registers. Note that the vector size ([7:0]) is located in the same place as the familiar single-instance register (between "reg" and the register name, "mem_buf"). The array size declaration then follows the register array name (in this case, [0:127]). You should note that verilog allows virtually any combination of numbers in the array size field. Thus, "[127:0]", "[0:1]", and "[1:10]" are all legal, the last being an array of ten registers. That said, memory implemented via verilog code is almost always declared as an array of either "[0:x]" or "[x:0], where "x" is the memory size minus one. The reason for this is that the logic that generates the write and read addresses is generally zero-based, i.e., for a 16-word memory, the address signals will consist of 4-bit values (0 through 15, i.e. 4'h0 through 4'hF).

The following is a simple dual-port memory. Data flows in one direction, entering from the left through a write port, and accessed from the right via a separate read port.

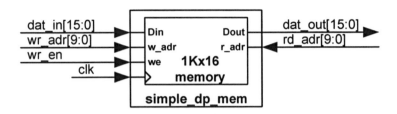

Simple Dual-port Memory

We will implement this as a fully synchronous memory, meaning that both the input and output data are clocked (versus, for example, that the output data changes as soon as the read address changes). This does not mean, however, that the write or read addresses are registered (otherwise, the write address would have to come one clock before the associated data to be written). Therefore, write data (dat_in) is presented to the memory during the same clock as the write address (wr_adr), but the read data (dat_out) appears out of the memory one clock after the read address (rd_adr).

```
/////////////////////////////////////////
// Simple Dual Port Memory

module simple_dp_mem
        ( clk,
          reset,
          dat_in,
          wr_adr,
          wr_en,
          dat_out,
          rd_adr
        );

    input           clk;
    input           reset;
    input  [15:0]   dat_in;
    input  [9:0]    wr_adr;
    input           wr_en;
```

```
output [15:0]    dat_out;
input  [9:0]     rd_adr;

reg [15:0]       memory[0:1023];
reg [15:0]       dat_out;

// ------ Design implementation -----

// Memory
//
always @( posedge clk )
  begin
    if (wr_en)
      memory[wr_adr] <= dat_in;
    dat_out <= memory[rd_adr];
  end

endmodule
```

Simple Dual-port Memory

So, notably, here we are representing the greatest quantity of FPGA logic so far with the least amount of verilog code. We see now how a register array ("memory") implements a memory; the addresses, both write and read, each point to one location (or word) in the array. If the write enable signal (wr_en) is active, at the rising edge of the clock the write data word (dat_in) is loaded into the register array at the location specified by the write address (wr_adr). Simultaneously, the value located at the location specified by the read address (rd_adr) is loaded into the memory's output register (dat_out).

Left to the fate of chance by ambiguity, this code would probably result in the synthesis software using the RAM block resources of the FPGA if available. Explicit direction can be included to direct the synthesis tool to either specifically use RAM blocks or specifically not use RAM blocks (in which case the memory is then referred to as distributed RAM). Each synthesis tool has its own format for these types of embedded directions, and the designer must consult the tool's documentation for guidance. In general, though, the synthesis directions are communicated via comments in the verilog code that include one or more keywords that the tool recognizes (strictly speaking this violates the premise of a comment). Here is an example—this directs the Xilinx XST synthesis software to implement the memory not as RAM blocks, but as distributed RAM:

```
//synthesis attribute ram_style of memory is distributed
```

This comment would be placed just prior to the memory register array declaration. Note that "memory" in the comment is the label of the register array in our code.

Note that although "reset" is brought into the module, it is not used in our memory implementation (in fact, it's not used at all, which is permissible in verilog). This is because RAM blocks, per se, do not have resets. If we wanted to implement the memory as distributed RAM, we would have to consult the vendor's FPGA documentation to see if resets are allowed. We should also note that the ascending/descending direction of the array size field is irrelevant. We declared the array size as "[0:1023]", but we could have equally declared it as "[1023:0]".

Finally, we need to address a troublesome point regarding the memory's operation when a write and read are made to the same address simultaneously. There are two possibilities: 1) the data that is read is the original value before the write replaced it (called "read-before-write"), or 2) the data is the new value that is being written (called "write-before-read"). Our code implies a write-before-read operation based on the simple fact that the write assignment comes before the read assignment in the always-block (reversing the order would imply a read-before-write). Newer RAM blocks typically accommodate either type of operation, but some older versions are fixed, and in that case, as the designer you would have to make sure your code matches (and that your design operates correctly).

Next, we look at a full dual-port memory, where both ports have both write and read capability.

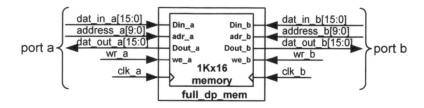

Full Dual-port Memory

As with the simple dual-port memory, this memory is fully synchronous, where write data (dat_in_[a/b]) is presented to the memory during the same clock as the address (address_[a/b]) for writes (when wr_[a/b] is active), but the read data (dat_out_[a/b]) appears out of the memory one clock after the address for reads (when wr_[a/b] is inactive). If you're not familiar with full dual-port memories, note that data written from either port can be read from either port—the contents of the memory are shared between the two ports. Note that we've also added a second clock, so that each port is now clocked independently (both ports could share a clock if independent clocking is not needed).

```
//////////////////////////////////////////
// Full Dual Port Memory

module full_dp_mem
          ( reset,
            // port a
            clk_a,
            dat_in_a,
            address_a,
            dat_out_a,
            wr_a,
            //port b
            clk_b,
            dat_in_b,
            address_b,
            dat_out_b,
            wr_b
          );

        input           reset;
        input           clk_a;
        input   [15:0]  dat_in_a;
```

```
input    [9:0]    address_a;
output   [15:0]   dat_out_a;
input             wr_a;
input             clk_b;
input    [15:0]   dat_in_b;
input    [9:0]    address_b;
output   [15:0]   dat_out_b;
input             wr_b;

reg  [15:0]    memory[0:1023];
reg  [15:0]    dat_out_a;
reg  [15:0]    dat_out_b;

// ------ Design implementation -----

// Port a
//
always @( posedge clk_a )
  begin
    dat_out_a <= memory[address_a];
    if (wr_a)
      begin
        dat_out_a         <= dat_in_a;
        memory[address_a] <= dat_in_a;
      end
  end

// Port b
//
always @( posedge clk_b )
  begin
    dat_out_b <= memory[address_b];
    if (wr_b)
      begin
        dat_out_b         <= dat_in_b;
        memory[address_b] <= dat_in_b;
      end
  end

endmodule
```

Full Dual-port Memory

For as much complexity as a full-featured dual-port memory contains, the verilog code is still relatively simple. Since each port operates from its own dedicated clock, we use separate identical (other than signal names) always-blocks for each. Whereas for the simple DP memory, each port was dedicated as either a write or a read, now each port includes both modes. Since each port shares an address for reading and writing, the question arises as to what happens to the read output during write cycles. In the case of this code, the operation is essentially write-before-read, meaning that when wr_[a/b] is active, the data presented on dat_in_[a/b] is copied to the read signal dat_out_[a/b]. However, whereas for the simple DP memory code the write-before-read was implied, here the operation is explicitly defined with the "dat_out_[a/b] <= dat_in_[a/b]" assignment inside the write "if" statement. Analyzing the always-block, we see that first the read assignment is made, and if this is not a write cycle (i.e., wr_[a/b] is not active), then we are done. However, if this is a write cycle, (wr_[a/b] is active), then the write data (dat_in_[a/b]) replaces the value that was read from the memory array on the read output signal (dat_out_[a/b]) before the write data is loaded into the specified address location.

But this introduces an important point. For the first time we see a signal being assigned values from within two different statements within an always-block (there were previously multiple assignments—the if-else and case statements—but they were all within the same statement). This is allowed in verilog, and the rule is that the assignment that is ultimately used is the last one executed. Of course, the "last one" may be different for each execution of the always-block (i.e., from clock to clock).

Although supported by the verilog language, assignments from within multiple statements should be used with caution. Even though the results can be predictably simulated, when synthesized into actual hardware, the operation may not always be what you expect. Additionally, the code tends to be more difficult to read with assignments made across multiple statements, especially in large always-blocks.

Speaking of multiple assignments, notice that, not only do we assign the output data from within two statements within the same always-block, but in this code we also make assignments from within two different always-blocks—assigning the memory with write data. This is normally a no-no, and would be as a minimum flagged as a warning by the synthesis software, and possibly as an error. In this case, though, it is appropriate since we are expecting the synthesis software to recognize that the two always-blocks go together to form one structure (the DP memory).

Verilog by Example

The dual always-blocks bring us to a last subject regarding this full dual-port memory: simultaneous accesses to the same address from the two ports (as implemented in the two always-blocks). This could be two simultaneous writes, or a write and a read. With the previous simple dual-port structure with one clock, we had the means to define what should happen—either write-before-read, or read-before-write. Here, though, because each port operates off its own clock, we have no mechanism in verilog to describe what should happen. In this case it is up to the synthesis software, and possibly the hardware fabric itself.

Lastly we look at a simple single-port memory—a type that is almost never used in FPGAs in any substantial way. The reason is that FPGA memory, whether RAM blocks or distributed, is based on d-flop registers rather than bone fide memory cell elements. Thus, RAM blocks inherently provide separate write and read ports; in fact, extra logic must be used to implement a single-port memory over a simple dual-port. We present this structure for illustration only.

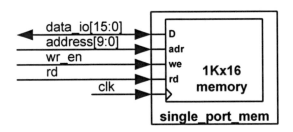

Single-port Memory

Data to be written is presented along with the write address and an active "wr_en" all during the same clock, while for reads, the read address along with an active "read" are presented during one clock, and the data appears one clock later. Since there is only one port, the data bus is bi-directional (input for writes, output for reads).

```
/////////////////////////////////////////
// Single-port Memory

module single_port_mem
        ( clk,
          reset,
          data_io,
          address,
          wr_en,
          rd
        );

    input          clk;
    input          reset;
    inout  [15:0]  data_io;   //new I/O type
    input  [9:0]   address;
    input          wr_en;
    input          rd;

    reg [15:0]     memory[0:1023];
    reg [15:0]     dat_out;
    reg            rd_d1;

    // ------ Design implementation -----

    // Memory
    //
    always @( posedge clk )
      begin
        if (wr_en)
          memory[address] <= data_io;
        dat_out <= memory[address];
        rd_d1   <= rd;
      end

    assign data_io = rd_d1 ? data_out : 16'bz;

endmodule
```

Single-port Memory

We introduce a new I/O port type; the "data" signal is declared as an "inout." This is verilog's way of defining bi-directional signals. If "wr_en" is active, data driven onto the bi-directional data bus (data_io) from some source external to the FPGA is loaded into the "address" memory location. The data at this location is also registered into "data_out", but this goes into the bit-bucket.

If instead of "wr_en", "rd" is active, then along with the data in memory being registered as "data_out", the active "rd" is also registered (i.e., delayed) as "rd_d1". During the following clock (when "rd_d1" is now active) the memory data being held in "data_out" is driven onto the external bi-directional data bus "data_io" by the assign statement. Thus, for reads, the addressed memory data appears one clock after the read (rd) control is active. You may remember that this is how the dual-port structures worked as well. When reads are not occurring (i.e., when "rd_d1" is not active) the bus is tri-stated via "16'bz"—meaning "16 bits of high-impedance 'z' ".

This assignment statement—using tri-state internal buffers—is the key method to implement bi-directional buses. The following diagram illustrates the tri-state buffer as it would appear in our code.

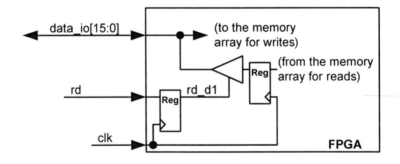

Tri-state buffer for bi-directional I/O

Managing Clocks

Synchronous design is synonymous with clocked operation, and virtually all non-trivial FPGA designs use one, and often multiple, clocks. It is difficult to understate the importance of ensuring sound, precise clocking. For large, complex printed circuit board designs, this is often a dedicated development sub-system—a design specialization. Fortunately, the FPGA manufacturers have invested commensurate effort in developing reliable integrated clocking resources. Their engineers have developed a sophisticated clock generation, management, and distribution sub-system for you.

The clocking resources in FPGAs can be grouped into two categories: 1) clock distribution, and 2) clock synthesis. We have now encountered two uses of the word "synthesis," but whereas our first instance pertains to the formal definition of the word, whereby the verilog code synthesis software "combines components to form a connected whole," clock synthesis, as we shall see, is more a process of creating modified versions of something (in this case, from a source clock).

The first category of clocking resource—distribution—consists of specialized FPGA buffers and routing facilities. Clock buffers are essentially current amplifiers powerful enough to drive a clock into the multitude of loads at far-flung locations with enough umph to ensure that the clock edge can arrive at each destination with minimum delay (and all at the same time, i.e., with no skew). In order to achieve this, the routing paths along the way must also be robust enough not to impose a load, meaning that they need to have sufficient metal. To this end, FPGAs have dedicated routing just for clocks.

Accessing these special clock buffers (often called global buffers) and associated robust routing structures can be achieved in verilog code by instantiating the clock buffer directly. Since the robust low-skew routing is driven directly by the buffer, it comes along for free. The following diagram shows a Xilinx clock buffer (BUFG), but each FPGA vendor has its own version. For example, the predominant Altera clock buffer is called "GCLK".

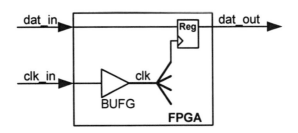

Clock Buffer

The following code shows the clock buffer instantiation, which looks like the module instantiations we saw earlier, because, of course, this is exactly what it is. The "BUFG" clock buffer is a vendor primitive, and is interpreted by the synthesis software as a black box (recall that the synthesis software simply passes these down to the vendor compiler, which presumably knows what they are). We recognize that once we begin using vendor-specific primitives, we are dedicating our code to that vendor.

```
////////////////////////////////////////
// Clock Buffer

module clock_buffer
        ( reset,
          clk_in,
          dat_in,
          dat_out
        );

        input           reset;
        input           clk_;
        input           dat_in;
        output          dat_out;

        wire            clk;
        reg             dat_out;
```

```
// ------ Design implementation -----

// clock buffer instantiation
BUFG clock_buffer_inst
    (
      .I   ( clk_in ),
      .O   ( clk    )
    );

// register
always @( posedge clk or posedge reset )
  begin
    if ( reset )
      dat_out <= 1'b0;
    else
      dat_out <= dat_in;
  end

endmodule
```

Clock Buffer

This example used an external clock input, but it is usually possible to drive internally sourced clocks though clock buffers as well. One example is when receiving a high-speed serial interface (e.g., Gigabit Ethernet), where the Serdes IP core recovers the line clock, which must then be used for portions of the internal operation.

Sometimes the FPGA will have special dedicated clock inputs that connect to internal clock buffers directly, further reducing delay and skew. For example, most Xilinx FPGAs have dedicated clock inputs that are labeled as "GCLK" (making it a bit confusing when comparing to Altera devices, since they use the label for their clock buffers). Since dedicated clock inputs are directly connected to internal clock buffers, there is no need to instantiate the clock buffer in the verilog code (although it doesn't hurt). Further, in order to even use a global clock buffer, you might have to bring the clock in on one of these special clock inputs. There's no getting around a careful look at the documentation regarding clocking requirements for the specific FPGA you intend to use.

Verilog by Example

Many newer synthesis tools will attempt to recognize clock signals that could do with a clock buffer and will automatically insert them for you (again, it doesn't hurt, and can only help, to make a direct instantiation).

A last word about clock distribution: newer, large FPGAs include increasingly complex clock routing and buffering resources. Particularly, due to the vast size and enormous quantity of potential loads, many large FPGAs include clocking subsections. These "regions" (often a quadrant of the die) host their own dedicated buffers and routes, where delay and skew can be reduced below what is possible for the global clocks (which are still available) that reach across the entire device. Some devices even include an even smaller sub-section. Often called "local clocks," these sub-areas are usually located along the periphery of the die and are associated with time-critical external interfaces.

The downside to this clocking sophistication is that when using these regional and local clocks, you introduce inherent partitioning to your design. You now have to be careful that all the logic associated with one of these sub-clocks can fit within the resources available in the sub-area, and more problematic, that all the logic can actually be *placed* by the complier in the sub-area. Conflicts arise, for example, when a signal that should be part of this sub-area is fed from or drives an external pin that is located in a different sub-area.

So far, we have looked at clock distribution that is sourced directly from an external clock. This is a common application, particularly where a single clock suffices for the logic operation, and the speeds are moderate enough that external signals can be clocked into and out of the FPGA with sufficient setup and hold times—up to perhaps 100 MHz. When the clocking structure and/or speeds extend beyond this, most FPGAs provide integrated PLL (Phase-Locked Loop) and/or DLL (Delay-Locked Loop) blocks that provide the resources needed for clock synthesis. PLL/DLLs provide the following functions in their role as the clock synthesis foundation, which we'll get to in turn:

  o phase alignment;
  o phased clock sets;

o frequency multiplication.

We start with the DLLs, the simpler of the two synthesis functions. The delay in the diagram below is just that, except that it consists of a series of precise delay elements, from which the propagating clock signal can be tapped as "clk." The phase detector compares the phases (relative edges) at the input and output of the delay, and can select the delay tap that creates the desired phase offset. Thus, for example, we could choose a slightly negative phase offset (i.e., something less than 360 degrees) so that "clk" is effectively moved back in time. Then it could incur propagation delay in the FPGA and be back to approximately where it was coming in as "clk_in." The clock edges at the FPGA's internal registers would be (approximately) synchronized with those on the circuit board.

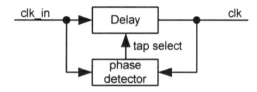

Simple DLL

But we can do better than this. Using the feedback path, we can arrange for the locked loop to automatically compensate for the internal propagation delays. If the phase detector in the following diagram were set to find a zero-degree phase difference, then it would select a delay tap accordingly. No matter how much delay is introduced between the delay and "clk," the internal clock would always be precisely in phase with the input clock (to within the quantum margins of the taps).

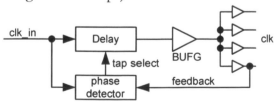

Propagation Compensated DLL

Thus, we have achieved the first point above: phase alignment.

Now imagine that we have multiple delay/phase detector sets. Suppose that the first is configured to select a tap to achieve phase alignment as described above, but the rest are slaved to the first, whereby each produces a version of "clk" that has a fixed (and convenient) phase offset—say, 90, 180, and 270 degrees. This is exactly what we often need in very high-speed designs—DDR and QDR memory interfaces, for example.

That knocks off the second point: phased clock sets.

We've dealt so far only with DLLs, and it's time to introduce the PLLs. The results are similar, but the means is radically different. You are probably already familiar with PLLs, as they have been a mainstay of electronics for nearly a century. The following diagram shows the delay unit of the DLL replaced with a voltage-controlled oscillator (VCO). Now, though, instead of selecting a delay tap, the phase detector develops a voltage (called an error signal) based on the phase difference. This voltage is arranged to provide negative feedback to the VCO—the phase offset moves the frequency of the VCO in the direction to bring the phase back to the desired position. If the phase detector is set to zero-phase offset, then you can see that this diagram functions the same as the previous DLL.

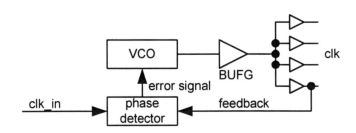

Propagation Compensated PLL

Since the DLL and PLL versions operate similarly, we will collect them together as a generic "Clock Generator" block and move on to talk about how internal clocks can be generated that have different frequencies than (but are still synchronized to) the original source clock. Frequency synthesis in FPGAs is accomplished in two steps: first, the frequency of the input source clock is multiplied up by some multiple amount (e.g., by 2, 3, 4, etc.), and then this higher frequency clock is divided back down by some other value. Although the up-multiplier is limited to integer numbers, the down-divider can typically also include half-values (e.g., 1.5, 2.0, 2.5, etc.). Thus, if we start with 10 MHz, and would like an internal clock of, say, 33.33 MHz, we could multiply up by ten, and then back down by three.

The following diagram shows how this is accomplished.

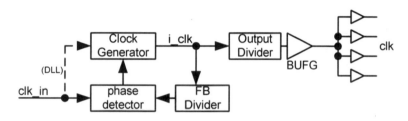

Frequency Synthesis

Since the phase detector wants to match the feedback clock to the input source clock, it must instruct the Clock Generator to create a higher frequency so that the FB Divider can reduce it back to that of the input source. (We haven't discussed how a tapped delay line can create outputs that are higher frequencies of the input, and we won't; you'll just have to take it on faith that this is so, as long as the desired frequency is an integer multiple of the source). The output of the Clock Generator is the intermediate up-multiplied clock mentioned above, labeled "i_clk" in the diagram. You can see that the multiplier value that is applied to the input source clock is simply the divider amount of the FB Divider. The Output Divider is just another divider that then reduces "i_clk" to the final desired frequency.

If we let "FB" stand for the FB Divider value, and "OD" stand for the Output Divider value, then the frequency of the final internal "clk" signal is:

clk frequency = (clk_in frequency) x (FB/OD)

The final step is now to mate the delay compensation of the earlier section with the frequency synthesis. In the following diagram, we've broken the path between the intermediate "i_clk" signal and carried it out through the FPGA clocking resources before presenting it to the FB Divider. As we saw earlier, this forces the "feedback" signal to be phase-aligned with the input "clk_in".

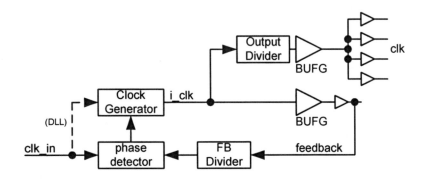

Frequency Synthesis w/ Delay Compensation

It is up to you, the designer, to make sure that the BUFG and routing paths associated with "feedback" match as closely as possible those associated with the main "clk" signal (the compiler software can often help with this via matched delays). The closer they match, the closer "clk" will be phase-aligned with the input "clk_in". We note that the FB Divider block will introduce some amount of delay, which offhand we might think would mess up the works, but it tends to be balanced by the Output Divider. The following timing diagram illustrates this.

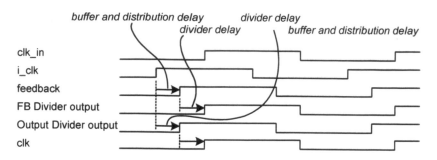

Frequency Synthesis Delay Compensation Timing

Note that "clk_in" and "clk" line up. This of course was the whole point. The output of the FP Divider also occurs coincident with "clk_in", and this is automatically a result of configuring a zero phase offset in the phase detector. Finally, note that "i_clk" is first in the pack, occurring far "before" the input clock "clk_in". This is magic of phase-locked loops.

Before we leave the subject of FPGA clocking, we'll compare DLLs and PLLs.

	DLL	**PLL**
jitter	The digital nature of DLLs results in some amount of small impulse-type jitter. This is rarely a problem with the internal digital logic, but can pose a problem for external interfaces that limit allowable jitter, such as communications links.	The analog nature of PLLs, on the other hand, exhibit much less jitter, and in some cases, a PLL might be inserted prior to a DLL for the exclusive purpose of reducing input jitter.
phase shift	Because of the same digital nature, DLLs generally have superior phase shifting capabilities,	PLLs offer some degree of phase-shifting, however, usually only in more general categories

	with outputs programmable to phase accuracies of just a few percent. Additionally, the phase shifts can often be programmed dynamically, meaning the FPGA logic can set them. Sometimes, even duty-cycles can be configured.	(e.g., phase quadrants). Also the phase shifts can not (yet) be dynamically selected.
operating frequency	DLLs can operate at frequencies that approach the practical limits of the internal FPGA logic, but there are some cases where their ceiling is a limitation. More bothersome, they tend to operate in ranges (e.g., low, medium, and high), which need to be configured prior to compiling (and are therefore fixed).	PLLs are able to operate at higher frequencies for those special cases.
lock time	can be long	relatively short

We didn't introduce very much verilog code in this chapter, but since it would be impossible to even begin many FPGA designs without an understanding of clocking methods, we might consider the material as a required entry ticket.

I/O Flavors

This is another chapter with very little actual verilog code, but also another chapter that's hard to ignore once you start coding an actual design. Long gone are the days when digital circuits were entirely TTL, and the only interface question was whether the DIP chip was "AS" or "ALS" ("Advanced Schottky" or "Advanced Low-power Schottky"). With the emphasis now on high-speed operation, a large part of the circuit board design often comes down to a process of careful coordination of specialized interface signals—making sure the I/O signals of the integrated circuits are compatible. FPGAs have a tally-ho leg-up here, since not only do most host a wide selection of interface options, but they are configurable on a pin-by-pin basis (almost), making them the consummately flexible partner in the circuit board puzzle. In this chapter we'll review the general categories and types of interface options available.

Signal interfacing has evolved into a vast menagerie of standardized forms—LVCMOS(3.3V, 2.5V, 1.8V, etc.), LVDS, HSTL, LVPECL, SSTL(3, 2, 18, etc.), etc., etc.. Among the parameters defined for each are:

    o voltage levels;
    o slew rate;
    o switching thresholds;
    o differential pair versus single-ended;
    o termination;
    o drive impedance.

Fortunately, most current FPGAs allow some amount of control over each of these. Additionally, many vendors also provide some degree of control over additional I/O attributes, such as:

    o inserted delay;
    o drive strength;

    o pullup/pulldown/keepers;
    o tri-state drive.

These various parameters are defined via three methods in the design of the FPGA: 1) instantiating special I/O primitives in the verilog code, 2) voltages applied externally to dedicated pins, and 3) design constraints.

We haven't talked about design constraints yet. Every FPGA design consists of two parts: the design code (verilog or VHDL), and a list of constraints. All of these—code and constraints—consist of text files. These constraints comprise essentially everything needed to build an operating FPGA that isn't included directly in the code itself. The constraints are entirely unique to the particular FPGA vendor, and many to the particular device itself, right down to the exact device package. The most common type of constraint is the pin definition—information associating an external device pin to an I/O signal. A 16-bit bus will have 16 different pin constraints. Every design has pin constraints as a minimum, but beyond these, there are many, many types of information that can be included. One major class is timing constraints, whereby you can define minimum and/or maximum propagation paths, I/O setup and hold, and minimum clock speeds. Discussions of these are well beyond the scope of this book, and are best handled via the vendor's documentation anyway. The third major class of constraints is the I/O definitions, which brings us back to these parameters.

We'll take a look at each of these and see how they are used and defined.

output voltage levels

Interface signal levels can range from 3.3 Volts down to less than a Volt. External input pins define the drive voltage. The FPGA designer must coordinate with the circuit board design to make sure the proper voltage is used for a desired standard. Note that I/O pins are grouped together in banks, where all I/O pins in the same bank share the same external drive voltage pin. Thus, all the signals connecting to a bank must share the same signal voltage level. We guarantee that this limitation will ultimately cause you much grief.

slew rate

Slew rate is typically categorized as simply "slow" or "fast". This parameter is defined, per pin, in the constraint file.

switching thresholds

Input voltage thresholds are for the most part defined via constraints. Each pin has its own constraint line, where the actual I/O standard is declared (one that is supported by the vendor). The constraint format is defined in the FPGA vendor's documentation.

Some I/O standards (those that define pseudo-differential input amplifiers) require a reference voltage provided by an external pin similar to that which establishes the output drive voltage.

differential pair versus single-ended

Differential pairs are defined by two means, both required. First, the two halves of a differential pair must be paired to proper FPGA I/O pins. The FPGA device hosts pin pairs that can either be used as one differential pair, or two single-ended signals. If used as a differential pair, these two pins further must be mated correctly with the positive and negative halves of the differential pair (if not, the logic polarity of the signal is reversed). Second, a differential receiver/driver black box primitive is instantiated in the code.

Single-ended signals are the default and need no definition.

Note that in addition to assigning the differential pair to proper pin pairs and instantiating a differential driver/receiver black box, a constraint may be additionally needed if the differential signal is to adhere to a specific I/O standard.

source impedance / termination

The very resourceful FPGA vendor engineers have developed means to digitally mimic source (i.e. drive impedance) and termination resistors. When used, these virtual resistors eliminate the physical resistors normally placed on the circuit board near the FPGA I/O pin. This has distinct advantages, particularly with ever-higher speeds and ever-denser FPGA packaging. With very dense ball-grid packaging, the resulting cluster of termination resistors means that many resistors simply cannot be located optimally close, resulting in high-speed stub effects.

The internal virtual FPGA termination resistors can be either in series or parallel. The impedance value (drive source for outputs, and termination for receivers) is set using two external resistors: one tied up to the same pin that defines the output drive voltage, and the other tied to ground. The value of these resistors (they have the same value) determine the internal virtual impedance for the entire bank as described above for output voltage levels.

Additionally, special I/O buffer black box primitives are instantiated in the verilog code. These may be dedicated primitives per resistor configuration, or the standard I/O primitive with additional attributes included—often simply the I/O standard being implemented. In all cases, as with other black boxes, these primitives will be unique to the FPGA vendor.

A common example is a differential receiver, where a virtual differential 100 Ohm termination is added.

inserted delay

Another tool developed by the FPGA vendors is insertable delays for both inputs and outputs. These are used to adjust setup and hold times, and are essentially the same as the external delay lines used since the beginning of digital design in the seventies. The signal passes through a delay path, and the output is selected from one of a series of taps. The tap selection (i.e., the delay incurred) can be fixed, or dynamically controlled. The latter is generally used when fine tuning very high-speed ports.

These artificial delays are invoked via instantiated black box primitives in the verilog code.

drive strength

The current drive of outputs can be controlled to some extent. The drive capability can be limited, often in increments of 2 mA; thus you can set the drive strength at 2 mA, 4 mA, 6 mA, etc.. In fact, the drive strength isn't so much limited, as enabled (how many drive transistors are used), so the actual maximum current available will vary somewhat.

Limiting the drive current is often useful in controlling transmission effects; limiting drive current can dampen the energy that might otherwise go into reflections. The downside is that too-low drive strength can result in too-slow transitions. Drive strength often goes hand-in-hand with the slew-rate control.

Note that the FPGA die can handle only so much power locally at the I/O areas, and there may be a limit to how many high-drive outputs are defined in any one group.

The drive strength is normally defined in the constraint file.

tri-state drive

Tri-state outputs were covered above in the Memories section, but here we note that, in addition to the verilog inferred method discussed there, these can also be invoked directly with vendor-specific black box primitives.

pullup / pulldown / keepers

These pullups and pulldowns are different from the virtual source/termination resistors discussed above in that they are actual resistors, albeit weak (high-value). They are not meant for termination, but rather to maintain an undriven input at either a high or low logic level. Pullups and pulldowns can also be added to tri-state outputs, again keeping the signal at a known level when the tri-state buffer is disabled (but allowing other external tri-state drivers to override the weak resistor).

Verilog by Example

Additionally, "keepers" can be added to tri-state outputs. These are nifty little circuits that hold the output weakly at whatever level was present when the tri-state driver was disabled. Handily, they work even when it's an external tri-state driver that has retired its drive. Since tri-state outputs are half of a bi-directional port, a keeper would in this case be holding the last driven level also for internal logic of the FPGA.

All of these weak input/output level-maintaining features are invoked by either instantiating black box primitives in the verilog code, or with attributes in the constraint file.

Before leaving the subject of special I/O, we will look briefly at a functional block that is a type of I/O, but also a whole complex sub-design of its own. This is the SERDES, which stands for SERializer-DESerializer, and like the memory structures earlier, is included in many FPGAs as a pre-designed section of circuitry separate from the programmable logic fabric. SERDES blocks allow relatively easy access to high-speed serial interfaces that otherwise might not be implementable in the FPGA at all.

At their core they are, as their name implies, blocks that convert incoming serial streams into parallel words, and vice-versa. But they are more than simple shift registers. The simplest ones facilitate DDR (dual data rate) and bit-slip operation (useful when the serial stream includes a framing pattern that must be located). The complex SERDES available in the larger FPGAs perform PLL-based clock recovery from the serial stream, and link layer functions such as 8B10B symbol encoding/decoding, comma detection and word alignment, and beacon signaling. Additionally, they include FIFOs for rate smoothing and PRBS generators/checkers for testing. Coupled with IP cores, they allow FPGAs to host such high-bandwidth serial interfaces as PCI Express, 10 Gigabit Ethernet, and SONET high-rate links. These sophisticated blocks perform as an auxiliary function in FPGAs what used to require an entire dedicated ASIC.

A Taste of Simulation

Verilog simulation is another subject that would require an entire (thick) book of its own to cover comprehensively. We will, however, take a passing look at how you can at least get started with simple approaches, perhaps useful for initial syntax checking and testing example code.

Simulation of verilog code consists of creating even more verilog code that exercises and monitors the code to be tested. This test-only code is called a testbench, and as the name evokes, is a virtual platform upon which your design rests and where virtual wires are connected to your I/O for stimulation and response. All of this is done under the control and execution of the hosting simulation software tool. To repeat, in order to simulate your design, you need some sort of simulation software tool. Luckily, "beginner" versions of popular simulation software are often available free from the FPGA vendors.

Firstly, we need some sample code to simulate. The following diagram shows a simple function, whereby if enabled, a series of 8-bit words are checked as to whether any two consecutive values are the same, and if found, are tallied. Note that the last word of a sequence block is held in the register and compared with the first word of the next series.

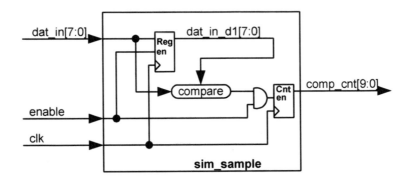

Sample Simulation Design

And here's the code.

```
/////////////////////////////////////
// Sample Design for Simulation

module sim_sample ( clk,
                    reset,
                    dat_in,
                    enable,
                    comp_cnt
                  );

    input          clk;
    input          reset;
    input  [7:0]   dat_in;
    input          enable;
    output [9:0]   comp_cnt;

    reg [7:0]   dat_in_d1;
    reg [9:0]   comp_cnt;
```

```
// ------ Design implementation -----

always @( posedge clk or posedge reset )
  begin
    if ( reset )
      begin
        dat_in_d1 <= 8'h00;
        comp_cnt  <= 10'd0;
      end
    else if ( enable )
      begin
        dat_in_d1 <= dat_in;
        if ( dat_in_d1 == dat_in )
          comp_cnt <= comp_cnt + 1;
      end
  end
endmodule
```

Sample Simulation Design

Now we need a testbench (verilog code) to test our design. What we require is some way to feed a series of 8-bit values to our "sim_sample" module along with an enable signal, and then check to make sure the tallied count is incrementing correctly.

The following diagram shows the pieces.

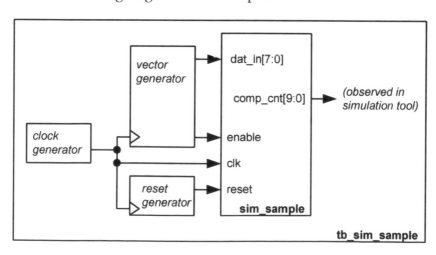

Testbench Using Embedded Vectors

Verilog by Example

We'll start with the simplest possible testbench.

```verilog
///////////////////////////////////////////////////
// Simple Testbench Using Embedded, Explicit Vectors

module tb_sim_sample_1
           (
              // no I/O for the testbench
           );

   // input signals to the test module.
   reg        reset;
   reg        sim_clk;
   reg [7:0]  dat_in;
   reg        enable;

   // output signals from the test module.
   wire [9:0]   comp_cnt;

   // testbench signals.
   integer i;
   integer j;

   // clock periods
   parameter CLK_PERIOD =  10; // 10 ns = 100 MHz.

   // ------ Design implementation -----

   // module under test
   sim_sample   mut
         (
           .clk       ( sim_clk ),
           .reset     ( reset   ),
           .dat_in    ( dat_in  ),
           .enable    ( enable  ),
           .comp_cnt  ( comp_cnt )
         );

   // generate clock and reset

   initial sim_clk = 1'b0;

   always #( CLK_PERIOD/2.0 )
     sim_clk = ~sim_clk;

   initial reset   = 1'b1;
   initial i       = 0;

   // reset goes inactive after 20 clocks
   always @(posedge sim_clk)
     begin
```

```
        i = i+1;
        if (i == 20)
          #1 reset <= 1'b0;
      end

    // feed stimulus vectors to module under test
    initial
    begin
      dat_in  = 8'b0;
      enable  = 0'b0;
      //
      wait (  reset );
      wait ( ~reset );
      @(posedge sim_clk);
      for ( j = 0; j < 20; j = j + 1 )
        begin
          @(posedge sim_clk);
        end
      enable  = 1'b1;
      dat_in  = 8'h00;
      //
      @(posedge sim_clk);
      dat_in  = 8'h01;
      @(posedge sim_clk);
      dat_in  = 8'h20;
      @(posedge sim_clk);
      dat_in  = 8'h21;
      @(posedge sim_clk);
      dat_in  = 8'h21;
      @(posedge sim_clk);
      dat_in  = 8'h33;
      @(posedge sim_clk);
      dat_in  = 8'h56;
      @(posedge sim_clk);
      dat_in  = 8'h56;
      @(posedge sim_clk);
      dat_in  = 8'h33;
      //
      @(posedge sim_clk);
      enable  = 1'b0;
      //
      forever
        begin
          @(posedge sim_clk)
          enable  = 1'b0;
        end
    end
endmodule
```

Testbench Using Embedded, Explicit Vectors

Verilog by Example

For a simplest of testbenches, there's still a lot of new verilog material to be explained. We start at the very beginning with the module declaration "tb_sim_sample_1". We include no port list, since the testbench has no signals entering or leaving—it comprises the entire simulation universe. Next we have the signal declarations, and they consist of two categories: signals that are inputs to the module to be simulated, and signals that are outputs from the module. The former are "reg" types since they are all generated as such, while the latter are a "wires" since they do nothing but make port connections to the module. The simulation software will use these wire labels for displaying those signals' simulated operation. In general, all inputs to the module to be simulated are declared as "regs", while all outputs are declared as "wires".

Skip over the integer and parameter declarations for now. Next we come to the instantiation of our sample module—the module to be simulated. Note that all the instantiat-ing signals within the port connection list are those that we declared in the regs and wires earlier.

Finally we get to some actual simulation activity. The first signal we'll generate as part of the simulation is the clock. The "initial" statement is new, and this is because it is only used in simulation. The first one in the testbench simply establishes the state of the clock "sim_clk" at time zero. Note that assignments inside initial statements can only be made to "reg" signals. As a rule, "wires" in testbenches are used only for monitoring simulated module outputs, or sometimes for connecting together multiple modules that may be instantiated in the testbench. Following the first initial statement, the next "always" statement generates the toggling clock. The "#" symbol is a delay indication, again generally used only in simulation (you may see it in a design, but that would probably be because the designer ran out of better design options). This "always" statement waits the amount of time indicated inside the parenthesis, then executes its contents (here, just the sim_clk assignment), then waits again. This goes on forever (i.e., "always"). The amount of time to wait is given as "CLK_PERIOD/2.0". In the parameter statement earlier, we declared CLK_PERIOD as 10ns. Since the always statement waits half that time, and since the clock consists of a high time and a low time, the total duration of the final clock is indeed 10ns. At the end of each half-clock wait time, the assignment statement simply toggles the clock polarity. "~sim_clk" means, "not sim_clk".

Next we generate a reset signal. First, we again establish the initial state, and here that is a one—this is because we want the simulation to start with the reset active. Next we initialize the entity labeled "i". We can see from an earlier declaration that this has been declared as an integer. Integers are very useful in simulation, but are rarely used in designs (they can't be synthesized as flip-flops or wires). In the always statement that then follows, the "i" integer is used just as a counter. We count twenty clock periods, then set the reset inactive. Again we encounter the "#" symbol—we're simply forcing the reset to wait a nanosecond after the clock edge before going high, avoiding potential timing issues.

Finally we come to the generation of the stimulus vectors for the data bus input. We use an expanded, multi-line "initial" statement. Initial statements are actually another form of the structured procedural statements that we introduced way back with the "always-block". As with the always-block, when there is more than one assignment line, they are grouped within "begin" and "end" keywords. Initial-blocks always start at time zero, and execution proceeds line-by-line to the end. Unlike always-blocks, initial-blocks execute just once in the simulation—when the end of the initial block is reached, it's done. Multiple initial-blocks all operate simultaneously (i.e., concurrently), and each starts at time zero.

Let's look at our vector generation initial-block. We start by setting both the data bus and the enable signal to zero at time zero. Note that even though the simulation executes the two assignment lines in sequence, since we haven't advanced time yet, they effectively occur at the same time (zero). But now we come to a new statement that allows time to begin ticking. When the simulation executes "wait (reset)", it literally waits until the reset signal goes active (true). Again, note that other initial-blocks (and always-blocks) are continuing to operate while this one is idle, waiting for reset to go active.

Verilog by Example

So, the two consecutive "wait" statements instruct the initial-block to wait for "reset" to go high (which, as it happens, is immediately), and then low—in other words, it waits until the reset period is done.

Next comes something we've seen before—what looks like a piece of the first line of previous always-blocks: "@(posedge sim_clk)". Not surprisingly, it works the same; the simulation waits until the next rising edge of "sim_clk". This is essentially also what happens each time an always-blocks loops around.

Following this is something you may have encountered before in software. The "for loop" in verilog is straightforward, with the parameters in the first line defining how many times to loop. Here we use an integer "j" for counting. The three definitions within the parenthesis, in order, are:

    1) the starting value of the loop counter ("j=0");
    2) the condition to continue looping ("j<20");
    3) the loop increment/decrement ("j=j+1").

For the definitions we've selected, our for-loop will loop 20 times (0 through 19). Note that we could have, for example, started j at 20 and counted down to 1.

But what does this for-loop do? Well, again we're just instructing the simulation to continue on a bit. But instead of waiting for an event (like the end of reset), here we count a particular number of clocks (20). We want the simulation to get a little ways from the end of reset before we start feeding valid data vectors. We could have also just told the simulation to wait a specific amount of time, but this method is cleaner—the simulation will operate the same no matter what the clock period happens to be. Also, this way the simulation remains synchronous—we come out of the for-loop just at the rising edge of the clock.

Time to feed vectors. For the first clock period, we finally set the enable active, along with the first data value (hex 00). Then, for each subsequent clock period we feed eight more values (hex x01, x20, x21, etc.). Note that since we don't do anything with the enable for this sequence, it remains as we left it—active. On the ninth clock, though, we de-activate the enable, ending this block of data vectors.

The initial-block ends with something of a contradiction. We stated earlier that an initial block executes once and when the end is reached it's done. Well, it so happens that there's no requirement that an initial-block actually ever *reaches* the end. The "forever" statement does exactly what it implies: it loops forever—here, simply performing a dummy act of setting the enable inactive over and over. Why do something inane just to prevent the initial-block from ending? Some simulation tools will sometimes halt when any initial-block terminates, even though other initial-blocks aren't done yet. Forcing every initial-block to proceed forever guarantees that all of them can complete. And there's nothing wrong with having a simulation that could theoretically go on forever—we generally tell it how long to run anyway.

So, what have we done with this simulation? We set the clock running, reset the FPGA, and then fed eight input data samples. Looking at the values we fed, we see that there were two instances of repeating data words (hex 21 and hex 56). In our simulation, we would have monitored the counter output ("com_cnt", perhaps within a waveform window) and would have seen it increment from zero to one, and then to two. Alternatively, we could have programmed the testbench to itself recognize that the count has incremented and display the fact on our monitor. This could be done via the "$display" simulation directive, but we won't go further with that avenue here.

The previous testbench is fine for a limited amount of data, but it obviously becomes quickly cumbersome as the amount increases to practical quantities (practical quantities for a practical design, that is—eight samples was probably fine for our simple sample design). The following testbench generates stimulus data vector values automatically using random numbers. It has the advantage that we can generate as many vectors as we like by simply changing a parameter value.

```
/////////////////////////////////////////////////
// Simple Testbench Using Embedded, Automatic Vectors

module tb_sim_sample_2
        (
         // no I/O for the testbench
        );

    parameter QUANT_VECTORS =   32; //quantity of vector
samples

    // input signals to the test module.
    reg        reset;
    reg        sim_clk;
    reg [7:0]  dat_in;
    reg        enable;
    reg [31:0] random_num;

    // output signals from the test module.
    wire [9:0]  comp_cnt;

    // testbench signals.
    integer i;
    integer j;

    // clock periods
    parameter CLK_PERIOD =   10; // 10 ns = 100 MHz.

    // ------ Design implementation -----

    // module under test
    sim_sample   mut
        (
         .clk      ( sim_clk  ),
         .reset    ( reset    ),
         .dat_in   ( dat_in   ),
         .enable   ( enable   ),
         .comp_cnt ( comp_cnt )
        );

    // generate clock and reset

    initial sim_clk = 1'b0;

    always #( CLK_PERIOD/2.0 )
       sim_clk = ~sim_clk;

    initial reset   = 1'b1;
    initial i       = 0;

    // reset goes inactive after 20 clocks
    always @(posedge sim_clk)
```

```
     begin
       i = i+1;
       if (i == 20)
         #1 reset <= 1'b0;
     end

  // feed stimulus vectors to module under test
  initial
  begin
    dat_in  = 8'b0;
    enable  = 0'b0;
    random_num = $random(1);
    //
    wait (  reset );
    wait ( ~reset );
    @(posedge sim_clk);
    for ( j = 0; j < 20; j = j + 1 )
      begin
        @(posedge sim_clk);
      end
    enable  = 1'b1;
    dat_in  = 8'h00;
    //
    for ( j = 0; j < (QUANT_VECTORS); j = j + 1 )
      begin
        @(posedge sim_clk);
        random_num = $random;
        if ( random_num[2:0] != 3'h0 )
          dat_in = dat_in + 1;
      end
    //
    @(posedge sim_clk);
    enable  = 1'b0;
    //
    forever
      begin
        @(posedge sim_clk)
        enable  = 1'b0;
      end
  end

endmodule
```

Testbench Using Embedded, Automatic Vectors

Starting from the beginning of the code, let's look at what's different from the previous testbench. First, we have a new parameter called QUANT_VECTORS. As we'll see (and as you've guessed), this parameter defines how many stimulus vectors we'll

85

generate for the test run. Next, we've introduced a new register signal, "random_num". As the name suggests, this will hold a random number. Nothing is different now until we get to the assignment of the stimulus vectors down in the initial-block. Where in the first testbench we specifically assigned a list of vector values, here we have a for-loop. We see that the length of the loop is defined by our earlier QUANT_VECTORS parameter. Each pass through the loop, i.e., each subsequent clock period, we assign a new value to "dat_in". Sometimes we increment the value, and sometimes we don't. Those times that the value is not incremented will result in our comparison counter in our design incrementing.

But what determines if we increment "dat_in" or not? As you've astutely guessed, a random number, of course. The expression "$random(1)" is a verilog system task. It generates a 32-bit random number. The "1" in the parenthesis is the seed, and is optional, but by including a seed, we ensure that each simulation run will be the same. Now you see why we declared "random_num" as a 32-bit signal. We're only using the LS three bits, though. Each clock period, there is a 1:8 chance that "random_num" will have "3'b000" as the LS bits, and the "dat_in" value will not increment.

In operation, you would monitor both "dat_in" and "comp_cnt" from within the simulation tool to confirm that the design is working properly.

Although efficient and easily understood, this testbench does have the weakness that the stimulus vector values are always incrementing by one (or occasionally static). In some designs, this limitation could be limiting, foregoing some value transitions that might be important—values stepping from 8'h55 to 8'hAA, to take one example. Often, it is better to incorporate more randomness into the vector generation. In the case of our simple design, for example, we could have simply used the LS eight bits of the 32-bit random number. Of course, then there would only be a 1:256 chance that we would see repeating values and consequential "comp_cnt" increments.

In the opposite direction, we might need less randomness and even more control. One example is a local processor bus, where we are simulating bus protocol activity—perhaps a microprocessor on the host board filling a configuration memory inside the FPGA. For specific control over the stimulus values we might come right back to that long list of embedded specific stimulus values. But there is a better way to handle long lists of vectors, a flexible and powerful method of generating stimulus vectors, whereby the testbench reads the values from external files, files that we've filled with our test vectors. Further, the testbench could even confirm outputs from the design by comparing them against additional result-files.

This is where we could continue if this book were a thorough, dedicated treatise of simulation instead of a concise introduction to overall verilog design.

Verilog by Example

The Rest for Reference

The best way to learn is to do, and in this case doing is designing. This has not been an exhaustive study of all the fine points of verilog, but by now you should at least have acquired a solid foundation to begin in earnest.

You'll need tools, though. The two dominant FPGA vendors, Xilinx and Altera, provide free introductory packages that also include free introductory modelsim simulation software. The web packages are quite large, so be sure to check your computer's resources against the requirements listed on the vendor's website.

What follows is for reference. As you work to mold lines of code into something that implements target operations, or struggle to reverse-engineer an undocumented design, peruse these pages for tidbits to help you towards your goal.

Expressions

Concatenation   {}
{4'h6, 3'b101, 5'h02} = 12'b011010100010

Replication   {{}}
{3{2'b10}} = {2'b10, 2'b10, 2'b10} = 101010

Arithmetic   +, -, *, /

Modulus   %
(4'hA % 4'h3) = 1
(4'hA % 4'h2) = 0
(4'hA % 4'h4) = 2

Relational   >, <, >=, <=

Verilog by Example

Logical Negation   !

Logical AND   &&
((3'b101 == 3'h5) && (8'h5 > 8'h4)) = 1
((3'b101 == 3'h5) && (8'h5 < 8'h4)) = 0

Logical OR | |

Logical Equality   ==

Logical Inequality   !=

Case Equality   ===
(4'b0x01 === 4'b0x01) = 1
(4'b0x01 === 4'b0xx1) = 0
where "x" is "don't care"

Case Inequality   !==

Bitwise Negation   ~
~(4'b1001) = 4'b0110

Bitwise AND   &
(4'b1001 & 4'b1100) = 4'b1000
(6'b111111 & 4'b1111) = 6'b001111

Bitwise OR |
(6'b111111 | 4'b1010) = 6'b111111

Bitwise XOR   ^
(4'b1010 ~^ 4'b1110) = 4'b0100

Bitwise Equivalence   ~^, ^~
(4'b1010 ~^ 4'b1110) = 4'b1011

Reduction AND   &
& 4'b1010 = 0

                & 4'b1111 = 1

Reduction NAND	~&

Reduction OR	|

                | 4'b0000 = 0

                | 4'b1010 = 1

Reduction NOR	~|

Reduction XOR	^

                ^ 4'b1000 = 1

                ^ 4'b1100 = 0

Left Shift	<<

                6'b101011 << 1 = 6'b010110

Right Shift	>>

                6'b101011 >> 1 = 6'b010101

Shortcuts

Shortcuts often end up being the long way round in the end, but for the record, here are some you might see in your travels.

Declarations don't have to be one-per-line. You can smash them together as much as you like.

```
input        sig_a, sig_b, enable_1, clk;
input [7:0] data_in, data_out;
```

You can also add assignments to wire declarations. Be careful here, though, because verilog requires that you make a declaration before you use the signal. So whatever is on the right hand of the assignment has to have been declared prior to this line (this is the main reason we generally locate all the declare statements before the implementation code).

Verilog by Example

```
wire    sig_a = reg_1 & reg_2;
```

If you'd really like to throw people trying to understand your code off the track, you can even smash multiple assignments on the same line (sigh).

```
cm = a | b; cg = t | r; wire s_a = cm ^ cg;
```


More Shortcuts

The Verilog-2001 standard (supported virtually universally) allows port direction and reg declarations to be combined with the module port list. For example:

```
module combine_decarations
    (  input        [7:0]   in1,
       input        [3:0]   in2,
       input                sel,
       output reg   [7:0]   out1
    );
[other reg and wire declarations start here]
```


Combinatorial Always-block

Always-blocks are not limited to clocked registers only. They can be used to implement combinatorial logic as well. The advantage is that we then have access to conditional statements (e.g., if/else), case statements, etc.. The disadvantage is that every signal contributing to assignments must be included in the sensitivity list. Note that some synthesis software is forgiving of missing signals in the list, but this practice renders your code potentially less portable.

```
always @(sel[2:0] or en or s1 or s2 or s3);
   begin
     if ( en )
       case (sel)
         3'b000:  outsig = s1 | s2 | s3;
         3'b001:  outsig = s1;
         3'b010:  outsig = s2;
         3'b100:  outsig = s3;
         default: outsig = 1'b1;
       endcase
     else
       outsig = 1'b0;
   end
```

Note that we used the regular "=" assignment rather than the non-blocking "<=". This is because the order of execution doesn't matter for combinatorial logic (as opposed to clocked registers, where it very much does, thus the non-blocking assignment).

Passing Parameters

We saw parameters used earlier as labels for state machines. Later, in simulation, we saw one used in the more traditional way as a labeled replacement for a constant value (CLK_PERIOD was defined as 10ns). Using a parameter this way is a convenient method to define a value once, and then use it multiple places. For example, in the simulation we can change the basic clock rate by modifying one quickly-visible line of the code. We can say that we are configuring the design via that value.

Any time we have a design where we might want to change values later—bus widths, for example—configuring via parameters is a very useful tool. What's even more useful is to pass parameters down into instantiated modules, and here we show how.

First, we'll create the lower-level module which uses a parameter to set the bus width.

```
module mux
   (  in1,
      in2,
      sel,
      out
   );
   parameter SIZE = 8;
   input [SIZE - 1:0] in1, in2;
   input      sel;
   output [SIZE - 1:0] out;
   // ------------
   out = sel ? in1 : in2;
endmodule
```

You can see that we've snuck in a new verilog feature: bus width fields can be labels. So, "[SIZE - 1:0]" is the same as "[7:0]". This is a handy way to quickly configure bus widths, and you'll see this used often.

Next, we'll instantiate the "mux" module within a higher-level module and pass the "SIZE" parameter down.

```
module top_level
   (  in_1,
      in_2,
      sel_a,
      out_a
   );
   parameter SIZE_A = 16;
   input [SIZE_A - 1:0] in_1, in_2;
   input      sel_a;
   output [SIZE_A - 1:0] out_a;
   // ------------
   mux
      #(.SIZE(SIZE_A))
   U1
      (  .in1 (in_1),
         .in2 (in_2),
         .sel (sel_a),
```

```
      .out (out_a)
   );
endmodule
```

In this top level module we've set the bus widths using a parameter (SIZE_A) in the same way that we did in "mux", but here they are 16 bits instead of 8. We pass this value down into the "mux" module via the line that starts with "#" between the name of the module being instantiated (mux) and the instantiation label (U1). If we had multiple parameters to pass down, each additional parameter set would be separated by commas. The field following the "." is the name of the parameter in the lower-level module (SIZE), and the field in the parenthesis is the value to pass down. This could be a direct number, or as here, another constant label (SIZE_A). The parameter value passed down overrides whatever was set inside the lower-level module, so the parameter "SIZE" in "mux" will become 16 instead of 8, which is good, since that's what we want in order to be compatible with the bus widths of the top level module.

Since a parameter label can be used to assign the value to be passed down, you can see that you could pass parameters down through multiple layers of a hierarchy, using the parameter name within each intermediate module (which itself is overridden from above) to assign the value that's passed down.

But there's another way to pass parameters down through a hierarchy—one that some designers dislike, but that you will surely see (or use) eventually. This is the defparam, and it explicitly defines both the instantiated name of the lower-level module as well as the parameter name used in that lower-level module. This is how it would be used in our top level module.

```
module top_level
   (  in_1,
      in_2,
      sel_a,
      out_a
   );
   parameter SIZE_A = 16;
```

```
input [SIZE_A - 1:0] in_1, in_2;
input      sel_a;
output [SIZE_A - 1:0] out_a;
// ------------
defparam U1.SIZE = SIZE_A;
mux U1
  (  .in1 (in_1),
     .in2 (in_2),
     .sel (sel_a),
     .out (out_a)
  );
endmodule
```

The defparam statement is located in this sample code just before the lower-level module instantiation, but it could be anywhere in the body of the code (although it would seem to be most sane right where it is). If used carefully, the defparam is perfectly fine. Each module in the hierarchy would have defparam statements that would define the override values for the parameters in the next module down. The potential danger arises because defparam statements are not limited to being located just in the module that's doing the lower-level instantiating, opening the possibility for unintentional and/or seemingly invisible parameter replacements. But we won't talk about this in any more detail, as that would be opening a Pandora's Box. As we'll see next, this is a similar problem that can arise using `define statements.

Passing `Defines

Like parameters, `defines can be used as labels representing a fixed constant. But unlike parameters, `defines are considered to have global reach, meaning that they manifest across layers of a hierarchy implicitly, and there lies both the power and the potential trap. `Defines declared within one module could override those of another, but since there are no explicit directions to do so, this could come as a surprise to you (potentially after many hours of puzzled debug). Further, which `define overrides which is not even necessarily easily predicted. Unlike parameters, `defines are directives to the synthesis tool (thus the "`" tick), and any particular `define takes the final value that the synthesis software encounters as it compiles the modules (this is a little confusing I know, since there is a separate, complete compile stage performed by the vendor tool). Granted, the synthesis or simulation software will probably warn you if it encounters two `define definitions to the same label, but often warnings are missed. So, the final value for a `define that has the same name in multiple modules depends on the order of compile. This is usually configurable in the synthesis or simulation tool, but can get messy all the same. Finally, what happens if the compile order is different between simulation and synthesis? Obviously the compiled FPGA will not operate as simulated. Very bad.

If you've gotten the idea that we're trying to make you nervous about using `defines, good. That said, `defines are very powerful and useful, and luckily there is way to use them that is relatively foolproof: pull all `define definitions into one include file (we'll talk about include files next). Now you only have to make sure that this top-level include file is at the top of the compile order. Using one master include file makes overall sense anyway, since `defines are really geared towards system-wide configuration, and it is useful having all system configurations collected together in one file. For one thing, different system configurations can be associated each with one specific file.

Finally, here's the syntax for defining the value of a `define;

```
`define NUM_CHANS    8'd32
```

Here, we're defining "NUM_CHANS" as decimal 32. Note that there is no semi-colon at the end of the line. The label is then invoked using a "`" tick. For example:

```
always @(posedge clk)
begin
  if (count != `NUM_CHANS)
    mem_array[count] <= dat_in;
    count              <= count + 1;
  else
    count <= 0;
end
```

A note of technical precision: parameters define constants, but `defines represent a text substitution. If the text happens to be a label followed by a number, then the `define operates like a constant. So, a `define has more comprehensive application, since it could be used to substitute words in addition to values. We'll see them again when we get to "ifdef"s.

`Include files

We introduced the concept of include files in the previous section. Like `defines, include files are communicated as a compiler directive, and so the form for invoking it is to add a "`" tick. Like so:

```
`include header_defs.h
```

`Include directives allow us to incorporate the contents of entire files into a module of our design. The most common example is to define system-wide configuration information, as explained in the previous section. Since the synthesis or simulation software does not treat this file as a module within the verilog hierarchy, it does not need to use a ".v" extension. Thus, in our example, we used ".h"—the common file extension used for header files in the C family of languages.

Note that the file name can be an entire path name (ending in the file name itself).

Note also that if the included file contains only `define definitions, the `include directive can occur anywhere in the host module—generally near the beginning for visibility. If, however, the included file contains any parameter or defparam statements, then the `include directive must be placed after the module declaration (i.e., after the module port list).

Conditional Compiling

Verilog includes a very convenient method of selectively including or excluding whole sections of code from a design at time of synthesis or simulation. This is yet another compiler directive, and it works very similar to the already-familiar if/else conditional statement. Here's an example:

```
//////////////////////////////////////
// ifdef example
`define bypass_scramble
module example_ifdef
    ( input                clk,
      input      [7:0]     in_1,
      input      [7:0]     in_2,
      input                sel,
      output reg [7:0]     out
    );

    wire [7:0]             in_1_a;

    `ifdef bypass_scramble
        assign in_1_a = in_1;
    `else
        assign in_1_a = {in_1[3:0],in_1[7:4]};
    `endif

    [ the rest of the code here ]
```

Verilog by Example

In the code, if the flag "bypass_scramble" is set, then "in_1" is assigned directly to "in_1_a", otherwise, in_1 is scrambled (its nibbles are swapped). The flag (bypass_scramble) is set via the `define at the beginning. If the `define statement is removed (or, more likely, commented out), then the `ifdef conditional flag is considered not set. Note that the `define statement could be in a different file (e.g., a configuration header file).

In our example we use only one line of code for the conditional compile, but of course there could be any number. The `else is optional, but not the `endif. The conditional options can be extended with `elsif (similar to "else if" statements). Note that each `ifdef and `elsif condition decision consists of a single `define flags, e.g., no Boolean combinations allowed.

Sometimes we would like to simply add some code if a flag is set, in which case we could use an `ifdef directive paired with an `endif. We might, though, also want to add code only if a flag is *not* set. One way to do this (and the only way before the introduction of Verilog-2001) was like this:

```
`ifdef bypass_scramble
`else
    assign in_1_a = {in_1[3:0], in_1[7:4]};
`endif
```

It looks like we forgot something when typing, but this works— if the flag is set, the compiler just ignores the whole directive set of lines. Verilog-2001, though, added the `ifndef. You can guess what this does. Here's the same directives using this:

```
`ifndef bypass_scramble
    assign in_1_a = {in_1[3:0], in_1[7:4]};
`endif
```

Another example of conditional compiling is the "generate" statement introduced with Verilog-2001. This allows you to selectively instantiate sub-modules, or create multiple sets, each with a different parameter attribute. There are three basic types: 1) simple conditional instantiation, 2), selecting among a list of possible module instantiations, and 3) looping to create a series of module instantiations.

Here's an example of the first type, the conditional instantiation. Note that we use the ordered-list form of port connections (we only define the signals of the instantiating module—the mating signals of the instantiated module are inferred by their position in the list)— not preferred, but this is generally how `generate modules are used:

```
generate
   if (UP_COUNT = 1)
      up_counter u1
         ( in_1,
           in_2,
           count_out
         );
   else
      down_counter u2
         ( in_1,
           in_2,
           count_out
         );
endgenerate
```

If the constant UP_COUNT has been set to 1, then the "up_counter" module is instantiated, otherwise the "down_counter" module is instantiated. Note that since the decision about which module to instantiate is made at the time of compiling (synthesis or simulation), only constants can be used for conditional decisions, not signals or variables whose value is only known during operation. In general, the constants used in `generate directives are parameters or `defines, probably residing in the header file we talked about in the previous sections.

The next type of `generate uses a case-type construct to select among a list of possible module instantiations:

```
generate
  case (OPTION)
    1: up_counter_frz u1 //freezes at max
        ( in_1,
          in_2,
          count_out
        );
    2: up_counter_roll u2 //rolls over
        ( in_1,
          in_2,
          count_out
        );
    3: down_counter_frz u3 //freezes at zero
        ( in_1,
          in_2,
          count_out
        );
    4: down_counter_roll u4 //rolls under
        ( in_1,
          in_2,
          count_out
        );
    default:
        static_reg u5
        ( in_1,
          in_2,
          count_out
        );
  endgenerate
```

The code should be self-explanatory. Note again that "OPTION" must be a constant (parameter or `define).

The final type of `generate loops to create multiple module instantiations:

```
generate
genvar i;
   for (i=0; i<=7; i=i+1)
     memory U ( read,
                write,
                dat_in[(i*8)+7:(i*8)],
                addr,
                dat_out[(i*8)+7:(i*8)]
              );
endgenerate
```

Here we have a module that implements a simple 8-bit memory, which we replicate and concatenate into a 64-bit memory. The first instantiation of the module implements bits [7:0] of the memory, the second, [15:8], etc.. Note the new variable type, "genvar". This is unique to the "for" `generate form, and cannot be used for anything other than the `generate for-loop indexing (e.g., it cannot be used outside the `generate structure).

We should note that the looping "for" version of the `generate directive can also be used to implement repeated combinatorial assignments directly.

```
generate
genvar i;
   for (i=0; i<=SIZE; i=i+1)
     assign diffs[i] = insig[i] ^ insig[i+1];
endgenerate
```

The SIZE-bit wide signal "diffs" contains information related to bit-changes along adjacent bits of the word vector "insig" (for whatever purpose this might be useful).

Finally, note that some synthesis tools have additional specific requirements associated with the set of `generate directives, e.g., some tools require named begin/end blocking.

Functions & Tasks

A function in verilog is similar to those you may have encountered in other programming languages: a function can have one or more inputs, but there are no outputs, or rather, there is virtually just one output—the value returned by the function. Functions are declared and defined within a module, and can only be used in that module (they must be re-defined if used in other modules). They cannot contain always-blocks, and thus are only used to implement combinatorial operations—generally those that are used multiple times in the code. Functions are called from an expression, and the returned value becomes part of that expression. There's no utility in performing a simple combinatorial operation in a function that you use just once, unless your goal is to fatten your lines of code.

Here's an example of a function that finds the location of the most-significant bit of a 16-bit word. The function returns a zero if no ones are found (i.e., if "word_in" is all zeros).

```
function [4:0] ms_loc;
   input [15:0] word_in;
   begin
     // find the location of the most-
     // significant bit.  Return zero
     // if no ones found.
     ms_loc = word_in[15] ? 5'd16 :
              word_in[14] ? 5'd15 :
              word_in[13] ? 5'd14 :
              word_in[12] ? 5'd13 :
              word_in[11] ? 5'd12 :
              word_in[10] ? 5'd11 :
              word_in[9]  ? 5'd10 :
              word_in[8]  ? 5'd9  :
              word_in[7]  ? 5'd8  :
              word_in[6]  ? 5'd7  :
              word_in[5]  ? 5'd6  :
```

```
                word_in[4]   ? 5'd5   :
                word_in[3]   ? 5'd4   :
                word_in[2]   ? 5'd3   :
                word_in[1]   ? 5'd2   :
                word_in[0]   ? 5'd1   :
                             5'd0;
       end
     endfunction
```

A couple of things to note: the name of the function is "ms_loc"; we define its size as [4:0] since this is also the value that's returned; it has one input, "word_in"; there is no "assign" command, since this is assumed for functions.

The next snippet of code shows how we might use this function.

```
     wire [15:0]  dat_wrd;
     reg  [3:0]   ms_bit;
     reg          ones_found;
     reg          blank;

     always @(posedge clk)
       begin
         if ( ms_loc(dat_wrd) == 5'b0 )
           ones_found <= 1'b0;
         else
           ones_found  <= 1'b1;
           {blank, ms_bit} <= ms_loc(dat_wrd) - 1;
       end
```

We call the "ms_loc" function twice, each time with "dat_wrd", which becomes "word_in" inside the function. If there were more than one input to the function, the order of their declarations must match the order of their location in the calling statement (i.e., functions essentially use ordered-list ports).

Verilog by Example

Note that we use a dummy signal "blank" since "ms_loc" is interpreted as a 5-bit value, while "ms_bit" is 4 bits (and register assignments should have matching field widths).

Although functions are often placed at the end of the module, they can be located anywhere after the module declaration.

Where functions are similar to counterparts of the same name in other programming languages, tasks can be compared to subroutines. Unlike functions, tasks can have multiple outputs, or even no outputs (or even no inputs). While called functions are placed in code where they are replaced by a single calculated combinatorial value, tasks are called to do potentially many different things, virtually anything in fact that the calling code could do—implement state machines, call other sub-modules, emulate a microprocessor.

The following is an example of a task. This task is simplistic (it could be implemented more practically as two functions, which would be more readable when encountered in the calling code), but illustrates the basic syntax.

```
task bit_scan;
   input [15:0] word_in;
   output [4:0]  ms_loc;
   output [4:0]  ls_loc;

   begin
      // find the location of the most-
      // significant bit.  Return zero
      // if no ones found.
      ms_loc = word_in[15] ? 5'd16 :
               word_in[14] ? 5'd15 :
               word_in[13] ? 5'd14 :
               word_in[12] ? 5'd13 :
               word_in[11] ? 5'd12 :
               word_in[10] ? 5'd11 :
               word_in[9]  ? 5'd10 :
               word_in[8]  ? 5'd9  :
               word_in[7]  ? 5'd8  :
               word_in[6]  ? 5'd7  :
               word_in[5]  ? 5'd6  :
               word_in[4]  ? 5'd5  :
               word_in[3]  ? 5'd4  :
```

```
                        word_in[2]   ? 5'd3  :
                        word_in[1]   ? 5'd2  :
                        word_in[0]   ? 5'd1  :
                                       5'd0;

        // find the location of the least-
        // significant bit.  Return zero
        // if no ones found.

        ls_loc = word_in[0]   ? 5'd1  :
                 word_in[1]   ? 5'd2  :
                 word_in[2]   ? 5'd3  :
                 word_in[3]   ? 5'd4  :
                 word_in[4]   ? 5'd5  :
                 word_in[5]   ? 5'd6  :
                 word_in[6]   ? 5'd7  :
                 word_in[7]   ? 5'd8  :
                 word_in[8]   ? 5'd9  :
                 word_in[9]   ? 5'd10 :
                 word_in[10]  ? 5'd11 :
                 word_in[11]  ? 5'd12 :
                 word_in[12]  ? 5'd13 :
                 word_in[13]  ? 5'd14 :
                 word_in[14]  ? 5'd15 :
                 word_in[15]  ? 5'd16 :
                                5'd0;

    end
  endtask
```

It looks similar to the function, except that there is no bit-width field associated with the task name declaration, since the task will have specific individual outputs, each defining their own bit-width field. The other difference, of course, is that there are two outputs in the task. Actual tasks will generally be much more complicated than this example.

On the face of it, tasks sound supremely useful, but there are drawbacks. For one, tasks, like functions, are defined within the module from where they are called. It's possible to imagine a situation where a relatively small section of code is repeated enough times to warrant the structural complication of snubbing it off into a task. It's less likely that you'll encounter a module where a large amount of code is repeated multiple times—the modular, hierarchical nature of digital design generally means that this amount of functionality would already have been allocated its own sub-module.

We should note here that tasks can be decoupled off into separate files and tied back into the calling host module via `include directives, and this would seem to open possibilities of using tasks elsewhere in the design, but since tasks can operate directly on reg signals in the calling host module, conflicts arise when the task declares regs with the same name (which happens more often than you might think). Again, this speaks for using a regular sub-module, where signals names are only locally valid.

For these reasons, substantial tasks are infrequently encountered in structural design (i.e., the code that's implemented as FPGA hardware). On the other hand, tasks are very popular in simulation, where the structure and use are more akin to software flow (linear progressions), and stepping aside to perform complex operations as represented by a few lines in the main sequence of operational steps greatly facilitates understanding the flow. You will find comprehensive coverage of tasks in verilog simulation reference texts.

Nesting If/Else statements

This is allowed within an always block, but if you do nest if/else statements, you should block each level with a begin/end pair. Not only will this make your intentions clear to others reading your code, but more significantly, the synthesis software will encounter no ambiguity as well.

Rest of the Rest

The following is a pot-pourri of remnant information that might be useful in your verilog endeavors.

RTL: we haven't used this acronym, but you will see it. It stands for "Register Transfer Level," and refers to a description of digital operation (i.e. HDL) that includes registers (and thus, easily extendable to counters, state machines, etc.). One of the primary functions of synthesis software is to translate RTL into gate-level interconnections appropriate for ASIC or FPGA implementation. "RTL" has become somewhat synonymous generically with HDL languages (verilog and VHDL).

Unconnected module input and output ports: it's okay to have the latter, but not the former. Unconnected output ports are just left blank in the instantiating port connection list (i.e., just the parenthesis, followed by a comma). Input ports have to be tied somehow. E.g., if a scalar input should be tied low, "1'b0" can be used instead of a signal name.

bit markers: an underscore ("_") can be inserted in numbers, and they are ignored (extracted) by synthesis. Thus, 12'b011010101110 can be pleasingly written 12'b0110_1010_1110. This goes for any radix. (Perhaps reason alone to choose verilog over VHDL).

signed values: Verilog-2001 added "signed" types to regs and constants. This defines the value as signed, two's-compliment. A signed reg declaration might look like:
```
    reg signed [31:0]  data_val;
```
and a signed constant might be:
```
    parameter signed [7:0] WIDTH = 8'h56;
```
Inputs and outputs associated with signed regs would be:
```
    input signed [31:0]  data_val;
    output signed [31:0]  data_val;
```

signed shifts: the introduction of signed values, required new type of shift functions—ones that know how to handle the sign bit:
```
    dat_val_shftd = dat_val <<< 1;
```
This maintains the sign bit, while filling LSB zeroes.
```
    dat_val_shftd = dat_val >>> 1;
```
This maintains the two's compliment integrity as it shifts to the right (extends the sign bit to the right).

Verilog by Example

Index

CPSIA information can be obtained at www.ICGtesting.com
Printed in the USA
BVOW04s1242151214

379143BV00003B/606/P